GIUSEPPE VERDI
and Italian Opera

GIUSEPPE VERDI

and Italian Opera

William Schoell

MORGAN REYNOLDS

PUBLISHING

Greensboro, North Carolina

Classical Composers

Johann Sebastian Bach
Antonio Vivaldi
Richard Wagner
Johannes Brahms
George Frideric Handel
Giuseppe Verdi
Fanny Mendelssohn

GIUSEPPE VERDI AND ITALIAN OPERA
Copyright © 2007 by by William Schoell

Library of Congress Cataloging-in-Publication Data

Schoell, William.
  Giuseppe Verdi and Italian opera / by William Schoell. -- 1st ed.
  p. cm.
  Includes bibliographical references (p.   ) and index.
  ISBN-13: 978-1-59935-041-7 (library binding)
  ISBN-10: 1-59935-041-6 (library binding)   1. Verdi, Giuseppe, 1813-
1901--Juvenile literature.   2. Composers--Italy--Biography--Juvenile literature.
I. Title.
  ML3930.V4S34 2007
  782.1092--dc22
  [B]
                                      2006026369

Printed in the United States of America
First Edition

*To Barbara McCullough, in thanks for her helping
to ignite in me a love of opera in general and
Verdi in particular*

Giuseppe Verdi
(Courtesy of Lebrecht Music and Arts)

one
THE MUSICIAN FROM RONCOLE

The life of Giuseppe Verdi was one of music and strife, beginning almost from his birth. Verdi was born on October 10, 1813, in Roncole, Italy, where his father, Carlo, operated a tavern and farmed. His mother, Luigia Uttini, also came from a family of tavern owners who had originally resided in the Alps. When Giuseppe Francesco Fortunio Verdi was baptized a day or two after his birth, the Verdis hired a local band of musicians and invited everyone back to their tavern for a celebration.

Roncole belonged to the Duchy of Parma, which at the time was part of the French emperor Napoleon's "Kingdom of Italy." Napoleon had taken control of Italy and named himself king in 1805. However, by 1814, Napoleon had waged a disastrous campaign in Russia that led to his ultimate fall from power. As a result, Italy, which had been relatively stable under his control, was besieged by troops from Austria and France, struggling for control of the leaderless country.

When Giuseppe was not quite a year old, Roncole was invaded by foreign troops, mostly Austrian. Over the next

Giuseppe Verdi's birthplace in Roncole, Italy

several days the French and Austrians alternately took control of the area, as the women and children, young Giuseppe and his mother included, hid in a church tower. Foreign troops not only raided homes and farms for food and booty, but often raped the women.

As a child, Giuseppe was known by the nickname "Peppino." His hair was tousled, thick and brown, and he had blue-green eyes. Although his family and their friends doted on the boy, he was shy. As Giuseppe grew up he became acquainted with virtually all of his neighbors. The Verdi tavern, which was constantly busy and full of people, was the center of Roncole social life, and beginning as a small boy Verdi helped his parents keep it running. In 1816, Luigia Verdi gave birth to another child, Giuseppe's sister, Giuseppa Francesca.

Giuseppe was not yet four when he began private tutoring in both Italian and Latin with the director of the village school, Pietro Baistrocchi. He was sent to the school itself when he turned six. It was during this time that Giuseppe began to be mesmerized by music. Hearing someone playing a hand organ in the street, Giuseppe begged his mother to let him out and get closer to the sound and instrument. His parents then bought him a spinet, an early kind of piano, which he kept for the rest of his long life. Self-taught, he spent many hours practicing on his spinet, acquiring basic musical skills.

When Verdi was a young boy, his parents bought him this spinet, which he kept for the rest of his life.

By the time he was ten, Giuseppe was a part-time organist at the village church in Roncole, San Michele Arcangelo. He also served as an altar boy, but did not have the same passion for religion he had for music. When he was eleven, while helping one of the priests serve mass, he was distracted by the sound of the organ. The priest, who had asked the boy to hand him the wine for the ceremony, was so irritated that he gave Giuseppe a shove that sent him sprawling. Giuseppe, mortified, cursed the priest, causing a small village scandal. This was the first of many incidents that would ignite the anticlerical attitude he maintained throughout his life.

Giuseppe's parents believed he could not get the fine education he was entitled to in Roncole and decided he should attend school in Busseto, a market town about three miles away. Busseto was much larger than Roncole and more sophisticated. It boasted two large libraries and a rich cultural history. It was the perfect place for a child of Giuseppe's gifts to be nurtured.

In Busseto, he boarded with the Michiara family. An inheritance from his maternal grandfather's estate helped to pay for his books and living expenses, and he received a modest stipend for playing the organ. On Sundays, Giuseppe walked back to Roncole to fulfill his duties as church organist. This was a difficult trek during the frigid winter months; one dark early morning he fell into an irrigation ditch and nearly drowned. With his studies in Busseto and his job in Roncole, Giuseppe had a challenging schedule at a very young age. But his parents adored their son and believed he should receive the best education at a time when many children could barely read or write.

Organist and composer Ferdinando Provesi was Verdi's first music teacher. *(Courtesy of Lebrecht Music and Arts)*

Giuseppe was enrolled in the *ginnasio* (grammar school) for boys, where he studied Latin, Italian, and other subjects. The director of the institution was a priest, Don Pietro Seletti. Giuseppe took his beloved spinet with him to Busseto and practiced it constantly. Sometimes he would play when the soldiers who were quartered across the street were trying to sleep, causing the captain to complain to the Michiaras.

Busseto was home to a *Società Filarmonica* (Philharmonic Society), which was frequently at odds with the church. Many in the clergy considered the music played at the theater, including the operatic productions, to be vulgar and heretical, and even pro-Napoleon. The clergy in Busseto thought many of the members of the Philharmonic Society were sacrilegious troublemakers.

One of the members of the Philharmonic Society was Ferdinando Provesi, an organist, composer, and music teacher.

Provesi held the post of *maestro di cappella* (music master) and was the church organist for Busseto. Provesi had been exiled after stealing from a parish treasury, but the influence of a wealthy family who became his patrons allowed him to return.

Carlo Verdi was told that his talented son Giuseppe should become one of Provesi's pupils. Under Provesi's tutelage, Giuseppe worked so hard at his music that his work in the humanities at the *ginnasio* began to suffer. When director Seletti admonished him for this, Giuseppe worked harder at the school and began sliding in music.

Provesi and Seletti were soon in a tug-of-war over the intelligent child. It was nearly too much for the boy to handle. Eventually, Provesi and Seletti decided not to work Giuseppe so hard, and he was able to continue his studies at both schools. He graduated with honors from the *ginnasio* in 1827, and then was free to concentrate on music. From the *ginnasio* he took with him a lifelong love of the writers William Shakespeare (some of whose plays he would adapt into operas), Alessandro Manzoni, and Vittorio Alfieri, whose patriotic writings on the need for a united Italy struck a special chord in Giuseppe.

Giuseppe began composing by his thirteenth year. "I wrote a wide variety of music," he recalled. "Marches by the hundred for the band, perhaps hundreds of little works to be played in church, in the theatre, and in private concerts . . . many serenades, cantatas (arias, duets, many trios), and several religious compositions, of which I remember only a Stabat Mater." Giuseppe also composed a new overture for Gioacchino Rossini's opera *Il barbiere di Siviglia* (The Barber of Seville), which became his first

The bel canto style of Gioacchino Rossini influenced Giuseppe's musical compositions.

piece to be publicly performed, preceding a performance of the work by an out-of-town troupe of performers. The overture was very well received.

Under the auspices of the Philharmonic Society, Giuseppe studied the works of several composers who would influence his musical compositions, especially the *bel canto* (pretty singing) Italian operatic composers Rossini, Vincenzo Bellini, and Gaetano Donizetti. He composed a cantata with vocal parts based on Alfieri's play *Saul,* in which the role of mad King Saul was sung by a Busseto tavern owner and amateur baritone. Giuseppe later decided that most of his early compositions

Antonio Barezzi, a prominent Bussetto citizen, provided both encouragement and financial support to young Verdi. Barezzi later became Verdi's father-in-law, and the two remained close throughout most of Verdi's life. *(Courtesy of Lebrecht Music and Arts)*

were childish rubbish and destroyed them.

Another important member of the Philharmonic Society was the popular and wealthy merchant Antonio Barezzi, who became a kind of surrogate father to Giuseppe when the boy was fifteen. Barezzi, who could play the flute and other instruments, was head of a music-loving family who lived in a spacious townhouse. Verdi became close to Barezzi's daughter Margherita, and fell in love with her —and she him—by the time he was seventeen in 1870.

That same year Giuseppe's family was evicted from the lands they leased because they were several months behind in the rent. Carlo Verdi had not only spent too much money furthering his son's education, but also on the property's upkeep and on charitable contributions. The Verdis moved into the tavern.

Giuseppe moved into the Barezzis' townhouse that same year. A murder had occurred next door, and Barezzi's wife thought it would be good to have another young man living with them. She knew that Giuseppe stayed up late to study and might hear if there was an intruder and could sound the alarm.

Giuseppe applied for a scholarship from a charitable organization in Busseto so that he could attend the music conservatory in Milan. His father, Barezzi, and Provesi all supported him, even pleading his cause to the Duchess of Parma, Marie Louise. There were several anxious months while Giuseppe and his family awaited an answer. Finally, he learned he would be given three hundred lire a year for four years, provided he pass an audition. Giuseppe would room with Giuseppe Seletti, the nephew of the director of the *ginnasio*. With his father and his music teacher, Provesi, at his side, Giuseppe journeyed to Milan.

Verdi was now eighteen and past the age of admission to the Imperial Royal Conservatory of Music in Milan. However, in special cases older pupils could be admitted, and Verdi and his boosters were sure this would be the case with the talented young man. For his audition he played a piece by the Austrian composer Heinrich Herz, as well as one of his own compositions, a four-part fugue (a composition in which one or two themes are repeated by successively entering voices).

To the amazement of Verdi and his admirers, he was rejected by the conservatory. At least one professor thought Verdi could never be anything more than mediocre, while others on the panel worried that their own teaching methods would clash with those of Provesi, the man Verdi had already studied under. Provesi died only a month later. Verdi hoped to take over the man's post as Busseto's music master, but he still had much to learn.

It was then decided that Verdi would take private lessons with a maestro in Milan. Barezzi agreed to underwrite the expenses, including room and board. Verdi's new teacher was Vincenzo Lavigna, a distinguished composer and conductor. Lavigna admired Verdi's compositions and was also surprised he had not been admitted to the Conservatory.

Verdi's attitude began to undergo a change. He was depressed by the deaths of Provesi, and his sister Giuseppa, who at seventeen had succumbed to a serious illness, possibly cholera, in 1833. Her death was a reminder that life was short, and the loss of Provesi's understanding and encouragement was a blow. He was also working hard on a mass for the Busseto Philharmonic. The grief and stress of overwork took a toll. Suddenly, living life to the fullest seemed more important than staying home studying scores in solitude; his music seemed less important than before.

Giuseppe Seletti, with whom he boarded, feared that Verdi was too tempted by all that the great city of Milan had to offer. The city was a cultural mecca with many theaters and restaurants and streets through which hundreds of people continually thronged. Verdi was living in Milan during the time of the masked balls, which attracted thousands of people in costumes who would dance, carouse, and party all night long. Verdi loved his music, but he was also a young man who wanted to go out, have fun, and meet people his own age.

Eventually, Verdi rebelled against Seletti's influence, and his rules. Seletti decided that he had had enough of the temperamental young artist, and he found a room for him with another family, the Dupuys. Verdi was not informed that he would be moving until the day arrived. Later Seletti denounced him as rude, arrogant, and altogether horrible. He was also angry that Verdi had shown interest in his daughter, when it was known how close he was to Margherita Barezzi.

The Dupuys also found Verdi to be a problem, and his teacher Lavigna urged him not to neglect his studies. Barezzi, who was paying for all this, reminded Verdi of his obligations to himself, his art, and to others.

Meanwhile, Verdi became acquainted with other young musicians in Milan, many of them members of the Milanese *Società Filarmonica*, an amateur musical group. Verdi gave his first public performances with this group at the age of twenty-one, playing the piano with the orchestra and serving as chorus-master. Verdi said:

> I was fresh from my studies and certainly did not feel uncomfortable when faced with an orchestral score. I remember very well some ironic little smiles on the faces of the gentlemen-amateurs . . . it seems my young figure, thin and not very fancily dressed, was one that would inspire very little faith in them . . . I was really very successful, all the more so because no one expected it.

Verdi received good reviews and performed with the Philharmonic Society again. He also won his first important commission, from a Count Borromeo, who wanted Verdi to compose a cantata to his lyrics. This piece, written in celebration of the birthday of the Austrian emperor Ferdinand I, was performed in Milan in April 1836. Years later the staunch Italian patriot Verdi would try to forget that he had ever composed a piece in praise of an Austrian dignitary.

Verdi hoped to get an important post in the city of Milan, but he was expected to return to Busseto and find work there. His patron Barezzi—not to mention Barezzi's daughter Margherita—awaited his return, as did his parents, who were still in mourning over the death of their daughter. The members of the Philharmonic Society expected him to take over Provesi's post as *maestro di cappella*. But there were as many people opposed to Verdi's appointment as there were in favor of it. The church did not want the post given to someone associated with the "sacrilegious" Philharmonic Society, or to someone with a theatrical background. Verdi's stay in sophisticated, secular Milan made his morals questionable to the parochial minds of the clerics. For its part, the Philharmonic Society was determined to appoint someone who favored music over politics. In the meantime, Carlo Verdi arrived in Milan without warning and insisted that his son come home with him. He knew that Verdi would never get the post if he remained in Milan.

When the father and son arrived in Busseto they discovered that the post had been filled by the church's preferred candidate, Giovanni Ferrari. Verdi was disappointed, his father was heartsick, and the members of the Philharmonic Society were utterly disgusted. Although Verdi continued working with the Philharmonic, helping to bring the organization to new glory, no one could forget the slight. Busseto was divided into two factions: pro-Verdi and anti-Verdi. It affected everyone in the city and engendered public brawls and near-riots. Fistfights over who truly deserved the post broke out on a regular basis.

Barezzi decided that it would be best if Verdi went back to Milan and continued his studies with Lavigna. He sent another protégé, Luigi Martelli, to room with Verdi, and paid Verdi to give him music lessons. Verdi loved going to the theater and cafes, and soon was spending more money than his patron intended. He did not neglect his studies, however, and Maestro Lavigna certified that Verdi had completed his courses.

With this certificate in hand, Verdi was even more qualified for the post of *maestro di cappella* than before—and his opponents were even more vocal. During a meeting of the city council, the entire Philharmonic Society walked out in protest. Things got so bad that Duchess Marie Louise forbid any music at all in the churches of Busseto. It was suggested to Verdi that he apply for the post of *maestro di cappella* at the cathedral in the city of Monza. In the meantime, he intended to return to Milan to escape the conflict. When the Philharmonic Society, which had argued on Verdi's behalf for months, found out that he planned to leave, its members became livid that he was threatening to take a post in another city. Verdi feared they would take out their anger on his benefactor, Barezzi.

Verdi was disheartened by the whole experience. "Just as I thought I was about to get out of so many of my difficulties, and earn an honest income, and be comfortable, I again find myself thrown back down into an abyss, from which I can see only darkness."

two
TRAGEDY
AND TRIUMPH

V erdi was twenty-two-years-old and anxious to get on with his life. He had no job, was dependent upon his supporters, and did not dare marry the woman he loved until he found security.

The Austrian Duchess Marie Louise decided to end the "civil war" in Busseto by holding a competition for the position of *maestro di capella*. Whoever won the competition, be it Verdi or Ferrari, would hold the post, while the other would continue on as church organist. While Verdi waited for the duchess to set the date for the competition, he gave an organ recital at the Franciscan church of Santa Maria degli Angeli. Both admirers and opponents came to hear Verdi play, and most were impressed.

Verdi easily won the competition, in which he had been asked to play the piano, read scores, and even sing. The judge, a maestro named Giuseppe Alinovi, told Verdi that he deserved to be a music master in London and Paris instead of Busseto. Verdi was pleased with this reaction but had mixed emotions

Verdi's first wife, Margherita Barezzi, daughter of Antonio Barezzi
(Courtesy of Lebrecht Music and Arts)

about finally acquiring the post. He would have to give about a dozen students five lessons a week each in piano, voice, counterpoint (the combination of two or more melodies), and composition. When not teaching, he would have to commit much of his time to the Philharmonic Society. This would not leave him many hours to work on his own compositions. Worse, he would not be allowed to leave Busseto except during his summer vacation. He had hoped to establish further contacts in Milan during this period, but little happened in the music business during the summer months.

He added to his responsibilities by asking Margherita Barezzi to marry him. This was a mere formality, as everyone had considered the two to be engaged for quite some time.

Recognizing that he would soon have a wife and eventually a family to support, he accepted the post of *maestro di musica*. He was relieved that all of the fighting over him was finally, hopefully, over. "I have been an impassive spectator in this long battle," he wrote at the time. "Everyone knows that I did not get mixed up with the factions, that I never fomented trouble, nor went against any of them, that I have never been so evil as to take pleasure in these battles."

Verdi and Margherita were married on May 4, 1836, which was also the bride's birthday. Antonio Barezzi held an elaborate reception at his home and invited friends, family, and every member of the Philharmonic Society. Carlo Verdi accompanied the newlyweds to Milan, where they stayed at the home of Giuseppe Seletti. Seletti had a marked dislike for Verdi and did not care for his father, either. However, he was a good friend of Barezzi's and loved his daughter. Seletti gave the newlyweds his bedroom during their stay.

Back in Busseto, the couple lived in an apartment that was a gift from Margherita's father. In Busseto and neighboring towns, Verdi was already a celebrity, and his new post only increased his fame. His services were in demand all over the region, and he held many well-received concerts with his students and members of the Philharmonic Society. But just as one civil war had ended, another seemed to be brewing, one that was even more personal and embarrassing for Verdi.

Barezzi had advanced Verdi much money for his studies in Milan before his grant became active and expected to be paid back from the scholarship fund. The organization that administered the scholarship, the Monte di Pietà, had only paid half the sum it had promised. This was because Verdi had completed his studies before the four-year period of the scholarship was over. Barrezi was so angry that he threatened to sue Verdi's father, who was having trouble enough paying off his rent debt, and the whole fiasco became public. Eventually everything was settled but it was quite humiliating for the young music maestro.

Composers during this period wrote symphonies and other long and short instrumental pieces, but the most prestigious and popular works were operas. Opera, a type of theater in which the story is told entirely through music and song, is an outgrowth of *dramma per musica* (drama through music) in which Florentine aristocrats of the late sixteenth century added songs to existing plays. By the end of the century the scenes between songs had been set to music as well, and opera was born.

Opera went through various stages until the early eighteenth century ushered in what is called the Romantic period. Romantic music was lush and more expressive and employed a larger orchestra. In its earliest forms opera was seen as an elite art only for the rich, but by Verdi's time opera was for everybody. The general public flocked to operas the way people today flock to movie theaters, and those who composed successful operas could become as famous and rich as any modern-day movie star; this was also true of star singers. Bel canto operas, which emphasized beautiful singing, were the most popular when Verdi came to Milan.

Somehow, despite the demands on his time, Verdi managed to complete an entire operatic score. He wanted to see the work, *Oberto, conte di* (count of) *San Bonifacio*, produced, but despaired that it ever would be. He felt trapped in Busseto and was sure that he had no real future if he remained there. No one wanted to risk staging an opera by an unknown.

Twentieth-century photo of Piazza del Duomo, Milan's central square

Lavigna, his teacher in Milan, had passed away, and Verdi had no more connections in Milan. This increased his sense of isolation. Members of the Philharmonic Society sensed his restlessness, and several of them opined that Verdi should seek his fortunes elsewhere. They had come to agree that with his gifts he deserved better than the post of music master in a small city like Busseto.

Further complicating his life, Verdi's post did not pay enough, especially considering all that he was required to do and the many hours it entailed. A year after their marriage Margherita gave birth to a baby girl named Virginia, adding to Verdi's financial worries. Verdi had always relied upon his father, his patron Barezzi, his teacher Provesi, and others, to play him up to influential people, with the result that he was too shy and inexperienced to vouch for himself. He finally mustered the will to go to the Teatro Regio in Parma and present his score to the director, but he was turned down. During a brief trip to Milan he approached an old acquaintance with some musical influence, searching for anyone that might help him, to no avail.

Verdi's son Icilio Romano was born in July 1838, bringing the young composer much happiness but also increased financial concerns. The following month all his monetary and career problems seemed insignificant compared to the death of his daughter, Virginia. The baby had not lived to see her seventeenth month. Verdi and Margherita decided to work through their grief by intensifying Verdi's efforts to improve his, and his family's, station in life. To that end, they traveled back to Milan when it was time for Verdi's vacation.

In Milan, Verdi and Margherita stayed, again, with Giuseppe Seletti and lived off funds loaned to Verdi by his father-in-law. This trip was no more successful than the last in getting his opera produced, but it did convince him that he needed to live and work in Milan and only Milan, which was considered Italy's major cultural center. The city, with its rich musical life, was in his blood, and he needed both its inspiration and its opportunities. Returning to Busseto, he resigned from his post as *maestro di musica*. He claimed that the income was too low to support a family.

Verdi had been told over and over again by many people that he was destined for greatness, and at twenty-five he had come to believe it. His compositions were met with approval, and some had even been published. He was sure that it would be the right step to stay in Milan and push for a production of *Oberto*. He was willing to give up a modest but steady job

Bartolomeo Merelli served as director of La Scala and presented many of Verdi's operas there. *(Courtesy of Lebrecht Music and Arts)*

to take the risk for his ambition, his family, and his art. Barrezi would subsidize him until he somehow made enough money to support himself, Margherita, and little Icilio. It was a gamble, but Verdi had no other choice that he could see.

A man named Piero Massini aided Verdi greatly when the young composer arrived in Milan. Massini was the head of the same Milanese *Società Filarmonica* with which Verdi had given his first public performances. Massini had influence with Bartolomeo Merelli, who was director of La Scala, the prestigious opera house in Milan, and convinced him to take another look at the score for *Oberto*. Pressured by Massini, Merelli decided to stage the show as a benefit for a society that provided financial support for widows and children of Milanese musicians. All of the earnings would be turned over to the charity. However, Verdi was assured of a full house to hear his work, as the annual benefit was always well attended.

La Scala, the prestigious opera house in Milan where many of Verdi's first operas premiered, still functions as a popular opera house today. (*Courtesy of Lebrecht Music and Arts*)

One of the singers scheduled to perform in *Oberto* would eventually play a very large part in the composer's life. This was a soprano who had recently made her debut at La Scala, Giuseppina Strepponi. Strepponi was a colorful character who had numerous entanglements with men and was the sole support of her widowed mother and siblings. She already had two illegitimate children and would have more. Her schedule was so demanding that while pregnant with the second child she sang right up until the very evening she gave birth, and left for Venice and another engagement almost immediately afterward.

As things turned out, Strepponi did not sing in the premiere of *Oberto*, although Verdi was already well aware of her and her work and would hear her sing many times. Merelli decided to postpone the opera for another season. One of the major singers in the cast was ill, and would not be able to return to work in time, among other problems.

This postcard depiction of La Scala opera house shows the magnificence of its interior. *(Courtesy of Lebrecht Music and Arts)*

As there had already been a few rehearsals, Verdi was crushed by this decision. He thought that Merelli had decided not to put on *Oberto* at all. Verdi was afraid he might have to return to Busseto and beg for his old job back.

Fortunately, he soon learned that *Oberto* had been put back on the schedule (it was no longer to be a benefit). But Merelli wanted some changes made. Verdi again appealed to his father-in-law for money to live on while he made the required revisions.

As Verdi struggled to finish the opera's revisions and provide for his family, his son became gravely ill. Icilio died of bronchial pneumonia in late October 1839. Verdi and his wife were disconsolate, but he tried to deal with his grief by focusing on his work. *Oberto* premiered at La Scala on November 17, but it was a bittersweet triumph for its composer.

Oberto is the story of a count who seeks revenge against the man, Riccardo, who seduced and betrayed his daughter, Leonora, and is now to wed another, Cuniza. Learning what her betrothed has done to Leonora, Cuniza demands that he marry her instead. But her father, Oberto, insists that a duel to the death is the only way to settle the matter. Oberto is fatally wounded by Riccardo, who flees, as Leonora mourns the loss of both father and lover.

Although *Oberto* did not galvanize the opera-going public, it did set Verdi on an upward path to success. It helped that the show premiered at La Scala, one of Europe's most prestigious opera houses.

Oberto received generally good reviews, but it did not get raves. The public and critics admired some of the opera's melodies, but it was also suggested that Verdi's music was too reminiscent of earlier composers such as Vincenzo Bellini; there was nothing innovative or special about it. On the strength of *Oberto*, however, Merelli offered Verdi a contract. It also began Verdi's long relationship with the Milanese publishing concern Casa Ricordi (House of Ricordi)

Giovanni Ricordi, founder of Casa Ricordi, published many of Verdi's operas. *(Courtesy of Lebrecht Music and Arts)*

and its founder Giovanni Ricordi, who would publish many of Verdi's scores and increase his wealth and fame.

It was extremely important for an opera composer to have his music published. Opera companies would buy the rights to produce a particular opera from the publishing company, which would then pay Verdi royalties. This was in addition to the monies the composer would collect from any house that commissioned or premiered a new work. In theory, at least, music publishers could also control where and for which company a work would be performed, and under what conditions. The composer's work would be copyrighted and this would, hopefully, prevent unauthorized productions of his work. Although most composers did not write their own librettos (the word portions of an opera), the composer was always seen as the most important creative force.

An opera could survive if it had a bad book and wonderful music, but the reverse was never true. As stories were often simply a framework for the music, the music was always seen as being more important than the libretto. Working from the composer's suggestions, the librettist would fashion draft after draft until the composer was satisfied that the words and different scenes would showcase his music in the best possible fashion.

The staging of *Oberto* was also Verdi's introduction into the often-tumultuous world of theater, which was considered rather low-class in many respects. Very famous actors, composers, and singers were treated with a certain degree of respect, but all others were considered to be at the bottom of the social heap. Impresarios (managers), agents, and other powerful people ruled the world of the artist and often decided who would prosper and who would decline. Verdi would have to learn that there were many, many factors to deal with to achieve success, and talent alone was not enough. A man would have to fight for every little thing until he became too rich, famous, and powerful to trifle with. Even then, there would be bitter battles.

La Scala was slow to pay Verdi his share of the profits that remained after subtracting what it cost to put on *Oberto;* fees for singers, musicians, costumes, scenery, and so on. Verdi also had many debts to repay. As he tried to compose his second opera, *Un giorno di regno* (King for a Day), about a man who impersonates the king of Poland with comic results, he hardly had enough money to pay his rent. Verdi was mortified that Margherita had to pawn some of her jewelry so that they could get by. He still found it difficult to humble himself before people, so he left it to others to ask Merelli for an advance on his contract, and therefore he never received it.

While he struggled with his work, Margherita became ill. Doctors were unable to diagnose her condition at first; although it was listed as rheumatic fever at the time, it may have been encephalitis. Verdi sent for her father when it became apparent that her condition was worsening. Antonio Barezzi arrived in Milan just in time to have his daughter die in his arms, on June 18, 1840. Barezzi took Verdi back with him to Busseto where the healing process could begin for both.

The loss of his sympathetic and supportive wife on top of the deaths of his children left Verdi in an inconsolable state. People around him were sure that he was going literally mad from grief. He returned to Milan only for the express purpose of telling Merelli that he was incapable of finishing *Un giorno di regno,* and that he wanted to stay in Busseto and give up the theater altogether. Merelli refused to let him out of his contract. *Un giorno di regno* had already been announced, and Verdi had already completed much of the score. It is likely that Merelli knew that finishing the opera would be a lifeline for the embittered and hopelessly despondent composer.

Un giorno di regno was a work of *opera buffa*, the Italian comic operas of the eighteenth and early nineteenth centuries. By the 1840s this style was not as popular as it had been during the heyday of Gioacchino Rossini, whose 1816 work *Il barbiere di Siviglia* (The Barber of Seville) was a model of the form. Although influenced by the bel canto composers such as Rossini, Verdi's style (as it developed) was much heavier and more intense, more passionate and dramatic, alive with sharp and violent emotion. Under normal conditions Verdi might have had trouble employing the light touch required by the genre, but operating while under a deep depression made it nearly impossible.

The result was that *Un giorno di regno* was not a success in any sense of the word. Several of the singers on opening night were ill and sang too low in order to preserve their voices. Although some parts were well received, others were declared derivative and roundly booed by the audience. Consequently, *Un giorno di regno* opened and closed on the same night. "King for a Day" had been all too apt a title, which some anti-Verdians gleefully noted.

Merelli assured Verdi that he should not be too disheartened by the experience and urged him to throw himself into his third opera. Verdi decided not to worry about how audiences reacted—they could not know what a struggle it had been for him to complete the work. From then on he said that "successes have never made the blood rush to my head, and fiascos have never discouraged me. If I went on with this unfortunate career, it was because, at twenty-five, it was too late for me to do anything else and because I was not physically strong enough to go back to my fields."

Merelli also helped with Verdi's decision to stay in the world of music. Now that the rest of the performances of *Un giorno di regno* had been canceled, Merelli needed another opera to fill those dates. He decided to put on *Oberto* again. Instead of slinking back to Busseto in defeat and remorse, Verdi stayed in Milan to oversee the new production. Under his contract, which Verdi tried to get Merelli to tear up, he still owed the company two more works as well. Verdi tried his best to care about *Oberto* and his contract, but the loss of his entire family was too great a burden.

Again Merelli helped by handing Verdi a libretto. Verdi loved it and knew that he had to set it to music. With sheer strength of will, a realization that he had to go on no matter what had happened to his wife and children, Verdi began work on his third opera. *Nabucodonosor*, popularly known as *Nabucco*, musicalizes the conflict between the Assyrians of Babylon, headed by Nabucco, and the Hebrews in Jerusalem in 587 BC. Like *Oberto*, *Nabucco* was a work of *opera seria*, a term applied to Italian tragic opera of the period.

Verdi hoped to have the new opera premiere at La Scala for the 1841-1842 season, but Merelli already had three new works scheduled and was afraid to take on a fourth. Verdi worried that if they waited for the following season, they might lose the first-rank singers that he hoped to have in the cast. Also, as Merelli had pushed him so hard to stay in Milan and continue composing, Verdi thought it an injustice that it would not be presented to the public that season.

Merelli did as he pleased and did not announce *Nabucco*—at first. But influential people, such as Verdi's preferred soprano Giuseppina Strepponi, interceded on Verdi's behalf. *Nabucco* premiered at La Scala in March 1842. It was an immediate success.

Nabucco proved to be Verdi's first hit. Audiences responded favorably to the music and demanded that certain numbers be encored. Newspapers reported that audience members left the theater humming the tunes. One chorus from act three, "Va, pensiero," became not only a kind of Italian anthem, well-known to every Italian even today, but remains one of the melodies most associated with the composer. Verdi became an overnight sensation, with all of Milan singing his praises as well as his arias. The promise of his genius, which had been recognized by so many in his youth, had been fulfilled at last.

Sadly, Margherita and his children were not there to share his long-awaited success.

Verdi poses with a copy of *Nabucco*, his third opera. *(Courtesy of Lebrecht Music and Arts)*

three
FROM MILAN TO VENICE

Although Verdi lost his family, his success with *Nabucco* attracted so many people that he had little time to dwell upon his loneliness. Some of these people wanted to use Verdi, hoping they might acquire some of his good fortune simply by associating with him. Others were devout fans of his work. And there were a few who became lasting friends of the composer. Verdi met many of these people through his work at La Scala or via his friendship with Countess Clara Maffei. The countess was married to an acquaintance of Verdi's, poet Andrea Maffei.

The countess gathered together important Italian artists, writers, and composers in her salon, where Verdi played cards and engaged in intellectual debates. The frequent guests included journalist Opprandino Arrivabene, who suggested stories the composer might want to set to music and directed other critics to Verdi's work; Francesco Hayez, a painter; poet Giulio Carcano, who was translating all of Shakespeare's works into Italian; and critic and librettist Luigi Toccagni. Tommaso

I Lombardi was Verdi's first internationally successful opera.
(Courtesy of Lebrecht Music and Arts)

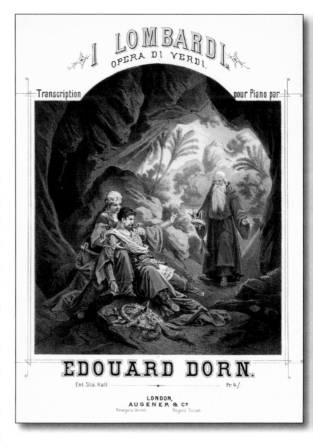

Grossi wrote the poem that became the basis of Verdi's fourth opera, *I Lombardi alla prima crociata* (The Lombards at the First Crusade).

Many of these people shared the same animosity toward the Austrians who were the ruling power in Italy. Every libretto Verdi set to music would have to be approved by the censors of the Austrian authorities, who would brook no anti-Austrian sentiments. The Austrians were so afraid of anything that might lead to public rioting or a revolt that they allowed singers at La Scala no more than three curtain calls for fear that lengthy ovations might lead to trouble. The first of many problems Verdi would have with censorship began with *I Lombardi alla prima crociata*.

The story of *I Lombardi* is a convoluted one centering on two brothers, Pagano and Arvino. Pagano tries to kill Arvino because he loves Arvino's wife. The two brothers are reconciled many years afterward, and Arvino leads the Lombards (an ancient Germanic tribe that had been living in Northern Italy since the sixth century AD) in the First Crusade, an attempt by Christian military forces to take back Jerusalem and the Holy Land from the Muslims. Meanwhile, Arvino's daughter, Giselda, falls in love with the Muslim prince Oronte.

The censors' objected to *I Lombardi*, claiming that it was sacrilegious. It was also deemed licentious, or too sexy. The police were instructed by Austrian-born Cardinal Gaetano Gaisruck (the Archbishop of Milan), who had examined the libretto, to deliver a message to Verdi, Merelli, and Temistocle Solera (who wrote the libretto based on the poem). The message read that *I Lombardi* would have to be heavily revised before they would be permitted to present it at La Scala. They were summoned to appear before the chief commissioner of police to discuss the matter, but an outraged Verdi refused.

Merelli and Solera told the commissioner that Verdi would not change anything. Further, they said that Verdi's reputation would suffer if he were to prevent the opening of a work so eagerly anticipated. The commissioner gave in after asking only for the change of one word—"Salve Maria" instead of "Ave Maria"—which was granted. Both *ave* and *salve* mean hail, but the latter word is more formal. The commissioner respected Verdi's genius and said he had no desire to hamper him. The night of the premiere the soprano was reminded that she must sing "Salve" instead of "Ave" or the police might storm the theater and bring down the curtain on *I Lombardi* for good. *I Lombardi* was a success. It was the first of Verdi's operas to play Paris and the United States, where discriminating fans also warmly welcomed it. But *I Lombardi's* major importance lay in the way Verdi and Solera weaved thinly disguised patriotic themes into the opera, which was both courageous and inevitable in a country that was getting more and more impatient with foreign rule.

Verdi's success inspired jealousy in some people. Operatic audiences of the day could be rude and noisy, and they were not shy about expressing their opinions. When *Nabucco* was performed in the opera house in Parma in 1843, one man in the audience incited others to suddenly interrupt the soprano, Giuseppina Strepponi, as she was singing an important aria. The man was arrested for causing a disturbance. The exact reasons for his behavior were not recorded. This was neither the first nor the last time that one of Verdi's operas was the scene of a melee in the theater. Also, though it is not certain, Verdi may have entered into an intimate relationship with Strepponi at this time.

Verdi had become so popular that he was getting offers from other prominent opera companies, among them La Fenice, which was located in Venice. Verdi had fulfilled his

Interior of La Fenice, the prominent opera house in Venice where Verdi's opera *Ernani* premiered.

This French advertisement depicts a dueling scene from Victor Hugo's *Hernani,* the play upon which Verdi based his opera, *Ernani. (Courtesy of Lebrecht Music and Arts)*

contract with La Scala, so he decided to accept a commission for his fifth opera, *Ernani,* from La Fenice. This was not disloyal; composers and other operatic artists were expected to accept assignments and commissions from other companies. In addition to *Ernani,* his recent hit *I Lombardi* was being prepared for an opening in Venice as well.

The libretto for *Ernani* is by Francesco Maria Piave and is based on a play by the French writer Victor Hugo. Ernani, a nobleman masquerading as an outlaw, is in love with Elvira, who loves him in return. But her guardian, Silva, and the king, Don Carlo, also love Elvira and desire her hand in marriage. This leads to bloody consequences.

Verdi's earlier operas, somewhat influenced by Gioacchino Rossini's later works, were epic in scope and featured massive choral numbers. *Ernani* was a change of pace for Verdi in that it focused more on individual characters. With Elvira's three suitors, Verdi was able to explore a musical

Francesco Maria Piave penned several of the librettos upon which Verdi based his operas. *(Courtesy of Lebrecht Music and Arts)*

characterization that was new to him. Going from highest male voice to lowest, the tenor was the young lover; the baritone was the conflicted, middle-aged king; and the bass was the elderly, self-centered guardian.

Verdi was taunting the censors when he chose to tackle *Ernani* ("Hernani" in the original French), as Hugo's play was already considered subversive. When the censors reviewed the libretto, they saw it as promoting anarchy in the way it glorified the bandit Ernani and made the king out to be a villain. The king reminded some of the Austrian emperor. They wanted many revisions: there could be no swordplay on stage; Ernani must speak more respectfully to Don Carlo;

French playwright and author Victor Hugo inspired Verdi's compositions with his subversive style of writing.

and the title had to be changed to distance it from Hugo's work. Verdi refused to do any of this.

Verdi was also having trouble with Piave, who did not seem to understand the special requirements of an operatic libretto. Piave gave certain characters too much to sing for too long a period, which would tax or defeat the strongest singer. "The lungs cannot hold up under this strain," Verdi explained. Some of the recitative (the sections between the separate musical numbers such as arias and duets) went on too long, which might work for a straight play but not for an opera. While important plot details could be expounded upon during the recitatives, there should not be *too* much time between arias. Verdi insisted on revisions. Throughout his career Verdi did not like to start work on a new score until he received the libretto in its final form. In his early years, he often could not afford the luxury of waiting, however.

While he was completing *Ernani*, Verdi was dismayed to learn that rehearsals for a Venetian opening of *I Lombardi* had gone badly. When the show opened in Venice it was a surprising disaster; the audience just did not take to it. It may be that they were reacting more to the singers than to the opera itself. Only one number received any applause. Verdi had extreme misgivings about the upcoming production of *Ernani* in Venice and wished that he had given the new opera to La Scala instead.

After the Venetian failure of *I Lombardi* Verdi tried to maintain as much control over *Ernani* as possible. He had learned the hard way how important it was to attend to almost every little detail himself. The libretto had to be perfect. Just as importantly, the right singers had to be hired. He knew that every detail of the production had to be perfect if the show was to succeed.

To that end, he insisted that La Fenice not use a second-rate tenor who had appeared in *I Lombardi*. He demanded that the premiere of the new opera be postponed if necessary until a proper substitute could be found. If his wishes were not acceded to, he threatened to cancel his contract with La Fenice and go back to Milan immediately. In Verdi's day, artists under contractual obligation had to hand their passports over to the management of any theater or opera house, and La Fenice was no exception. The management refused to release Verdi's passport, but they did allow him to investigate some other tenors who might be more appropriate for *Ernani*.

As the night of the premiere approached, Verdi was nervous and miserable. *Ernani* would be presented to the public for the first time under the worst possible conditions. Verdi was still working on the score and orchestrating the music up until the opening night. Still stinging from the reception given *I Lombardi*, Verdi wondered how the blunt and demanding Venetian public would react to his new work. The audience at La Fenice had reacted so negatively and violently to a new work by another composer that the singers nearly had to run for their lives and La Fenice's director temporarily resigned.

On opening night the new tenor that had been hired began a loud argument with the management that left him too hoarse to give a credible performance. The soprano kept pestering Verdi for more arias that would showcase her ability only hours before the premiere. There were problems with the scenery and costumes, some of which had not even been delivered. The audience seemed restless, and to Verdi, at least, out for blood. None of the singers seemed good enough. Verdi readied himself to flee Venice at the earliest opportunity.

Luckily the audience applauded after each aria and called for Verdi to take a bow after each act. *Ernani* was by no means as successful as *Nabucco*, but it was not a disaster, either. In fact, a small, adoring band playing Verdi's music followed him back to his quarters. Verdi was invited into the homes of prominent Venetians, both artists and patrons of the arts. He also began a brief relationship with a Venetian woman whose exact identity has never been known. He might not have been the hero that he was in Milan, but he certainly had many admirers.

Eventually *Ernani* played many other cities in Italy and in other countries as well. It was the first of Verdi's operas to be performed in Britain, and its success there and elsewhere did much to further his international reputation.

Following his success with *Ernani*, Verdi returned home. He used much of his money to buy a sixty-two acre farm called Il Pugaro, near Busseto. When his parents moved onto the property, people mistakenly assumed that Verdi had turned the farm over to them. Verdi was still the owner, however. In addition to a farm, he also acquired a protégé named Emanuele Muzio, who was recommended to him by his former patron and father-in-law Antonio Barezzi. Barezzi had also been a patron to Muzio, supporting the young man as he studied music and began his career.

Muzio had been awarded a grant to study music in Milan, and Barezzi wanted Verdi to take the younger man under his wing. Muzio would become an assistant to Verdi as well as his pupil. Over time, they became close friends. Verdi would use Muzio as his eyes and ears when he himself could not travel to oversee a particular production of one of his operas.

Verdi's success meant that he was busier than ever, and as such, he needed an assistant. There was a lot more to being an opera composer than just composing. Verdi and his peers had to deal with impresarios, librettists, contracts, and music publishers, as well as difficult singers and conductors. The greatest nightmare of all opera composers was that inappropriate vocalists and indifferent conductors who played at the wrong tempo could ruin their carefully crafted works. There were also many egos that needed nurturing. Everyone involved with a production wanted to shine and make his or her mark. The composer had to fight to make certain that his basic vision remained unchanged. This was not an easy task.

Even in these early days, people who wanted to praise, hire, exploit, or interview him constantly besieged Verdi, seen as a rising star. Muzio did his best to act as a buffer between these people and Verdi, who was always desperately trying to meet one deadline or another. He worked on his scores from eight in the morning until after midnight almost every day, with only a two-hour lunch break, if that long. His work was made increasingly difficult by all the interruptions and the demands made upon him to attend a function or compose some song for an event. Despite Muzio's assistance, the continual pressure eventually created serious health problems for Verdi. He suffered most of his adult life from rheumatism (painfully inflamed muscles and joints), neuralgia (severe pain along the course of a nerve), and various debilitating stomach ailments.

Verdi's next work was *I due Foscari* (The Two Foscari), from eighteenth-century British poet Lord Byron's tragedy, about a Venetian family suffering because of the hatred of one man, Loredano. With this opera Verdi took musical characterization to another level, introducing each character with his or her own orchestral theme, which also underlined the character's subsequent appearances.

I due Foscari premiered in Rome in November 1844. The opening night reception was not all that Verdi hoped for, although he received an ovation. Some blamed the high ticket prices for the audience's grumbling, others thought the singers were not at their best. In any case, *I due Foscari* did not become as popular as Verdi's previous works. Verdi himself believed that there was a lack of variety in the music and that the subject matter was too grim.

Verdi returned to La Scala for his next opera, *Giovanna d'Arco* (Joan of Arc). For the story of the French heroine and martyr, Verdi worked tirelessly not only on the score but on all aspects of the production. The standards at the famed opera house had deteriorated to a shocking degree, and Verdi knew he had to take charge. This pitted him against the director, Merelli. Although many of Verdi's subsequent operas would play La Scala, there would not be a premiere of a new work by Verdi for more than twenty years—at Verdi's insistence.

Verdi wrote a detailed letter of instruction for the conductor. As often occurred, there were problems with the singers. The soprano singing the lead role was past her prime and extremely upset over her inability to deliver all that the music required of her. The tenor was rumored to be pro-Austrian and was afraid he might be jeered the moment he set foot on the stage. In spite of these problems, the show was another hit for Verdi.

Along with Milan's La Scala and Venice's La Fenice, the Teatro San Carlo in Naples was one of the three most prestigious opera houses in Italy. Verdi was eager to have his work on display at this house, so he accepted an offer to produce his next work, *Alzira*, in Naples. He composed the music during a difficult period, when he was beset with both physical and emotional problems.

In spite of the many new friends and acquaintances Verdi had made in Milan, they could not replace his wife and children. Therefore it worried and angered him that he received infrequent letters from his friends back in Busseto, especially his former father-in-law Barezzi. Barezzi was his one link to the late Margherita. For their part, it may have seemed to the friends in Busseto that the now famous Giuseppe Verdi had gone on to a new and busy life that they had no real part in. They may not have realized how lonely he was when each day's work was done.

As Verdi rushed to finish the score of *Alzira*, he could not know that there was to be at least one more dispute in Busseto and a battle of a different kind in Naples. There was also about to be a revolution in Milan.

four
MACBETH AND CONFLICT

Back in Busseto there was more intrigue brewing between the clergy and the Philharmonic Society. Emanuele Muzio, Verdi's assistant and pupil, had submitted some marches to be performed by the Philharmonic. Admiring these pieces, Verdi had even helped Muzio with the orchestrations. Verdi was convinced the marches were good and would be easy for the Philharmonic to play. But Muzio's compositions became just another casualty in yet another battle over who would take over Verdi's old post of music master.

Just as there had been opposing factions supporting Verdi and Ferrari, now there were two groups in favor of Muzio or the clergy's candidate, an organist named Enrico Landi. Landi was another protege of Barezzi. While all the members of the Philharmonic Society had supported Verdi, Muzio did not have the same luck. Many important Society members preferred Landi for the post. These members therefore decided that Muzio's marches were incomprehensible and impossible to play. Verdi was more enraged by this snub than Muzio was.

Emanuele Muzio, Verdi's assistant and pupil (*Courtesy of Lebrecht Music and Arts*)

Then there was the controversy over Busseto's new opera house, which the Society wanted to name after Verdi. They expected Verdi to write a new opera specifically for Busseto, and to bring along some famous singers to appear in it as well. Verdi later regretted being gracious and suggesting he might do so. He wrote Barezzi that it would be difficult enough to complete the works he was already commissioned to compose, and that one could hardly expect famous singers to appear in the small city of Busseto. This would mean that they would have to cancel a much higher-paying engagement in Milan or Naples.

Verdi also did not like the idea of the opera house being named after him: "it makes me sound like an ambitious man who wants to have a theatre named after him with a bust [in the lobby]. . . . And most Italians know from experience that I oppose this publicity whenever I can." Verdi had a healthy ego, but he did not want to be perceived as vain and superior. For many years to come the business with Busseto's opera house was a source of great frustration.

Verdi continued writing and overseeing the staging of new works. Premiering in Naples in 1845, *Alzira* is the story of an Inca princess who is loved by two rivals: the Peruvian governor Gusmano and an Indian chief named Zamoro. The libretto was by Salvatore Cammarano. Although greeted warmly by crowds of admirers in Naples, there were factions working against Verdi behind the scenes. The director of the Neapolitan conservatory of music was Saverio Mercadante, who was also a highly regarded composer of such operas as 1837's *Il giuramento* (The Oath) and 1843's *Il reggente* (The Regent). Naples was Mercadante's town, and many of his fans resented Verdi's presence. The fact that there was a vocal pro-Verdi faction only made the Mercadante loyalists angrier.

It was not uncommon in those days for groups of people, known as "claques," to be hired to applaud one singer or hiss another. Loyalties, as well as positive or negative reactions, could be bought for the right price. Verdi learned that one soprano he'd had bounced from the production of *Alzira* was paying out bribes to newspapers. "It is certain that the newspapers will say all kinds of bad things," Verdi noted in a letter to one editor, "now that La Bishop has increased her monthly payments to those gentlemen, since I do not want her in my opera."

The Neapolitan audience applauded certain parts of *Alzira*, but for the rest of the time they were silent. The excellent singers received most of the kind words about the opera, which was not well reviewed in the local press.

Verdi was so disheartened by the whole experience in Naples that he told many of his friends and colleagues that he would retire from opera as soon as he had fulfilled all of his commitments. But this would not be the first nor last time that the great composer threatened to permanently put down his pen. Opera—and the fire of creativity—was in Verdi's blood more than he wanted to admit. Besides, he wasn't yet thirty. Many works were still ahead of him.

A young Giuseppe Verdi poses with a pen in his hand. *(Courtesy of Lebrecht Music and Arts)*

Instead of retiring, Verdi bought a townhouse in Milan, settled in, and began work on his next opera. Verdi's inspiration for the work came from Andrea Maffei, who had directed Verdi's attention to a play about Attila the Hun by Zacharias Werner. Verdi based *Attila,* his musical examination of the life of the great conqueror, on Werner's play. The opera premiered at La Fenice in Venice in March 1846. The opening night was beset with the singers' vocal problems and an accident with some stage smoke that sent patrons into a brief fit of coughing. The reception was cool at first, but by the third performance *Attila* was garnering bravos. Bartolomeo Merelli wanted to do a production of *Attila* at La Scala, but Verdi was angered by negative remarks the director had made about the score. He asked his publisher to charge the theater an exorbitant amount for the rights to stage the work. Eventually Merelli appealed to the chief of police to get the fees lowered. By this time, Verdi had entered into a contract with the publisher Francesco Lucca (his contract with Ricordi was not exclusive), to whom he promised a number of scores.

Verdi's deal with Lucca was quite different from his arrangement with Ricordi, who only paid for publishing rights. For a fee, Lucca would *own* the score and have the right to submit it to the opera house of his choosing. In other words, Verdi would be composing an opera for Lucca instead of for a particular company. Ricordi might try to interest other opera houses in one of Verdi's works after it had already premiered; Lucca would arrange for the premiere itself. This was one of the first contracts of its kind for an opera composer and it was considered a mark of high prestige. Verdi would make more money and someone else would deal with the opera houses on various mundane matters. Verdi would not be in business with Lucca for long, however. He came to despise the publisher, whom he found "insensitive, mean, demanding toward me . . . I cannot pardon an insult to which I cannot respond."

Even more, Verdi hated conductors, impresarios, and singers who tried to impose their own will on his work, making changes in tempo, emphasis, and even orchestration to suit their own needs. Verdi did everything he could to make sure that people he viewed as insensitive boors did not dilute or destroy the impact of his music. Verdi's health was poor during this period. Much of the trouble was caused by the emotional stress he underwent as he hurried to finish an opera, and then worried over every little detail of the production. Even as he took a rest at a spa, he worried over why Barezzi was not writing to him. Despite—or because of—all the many friends, sycophants, hangers-on, and colleagues that he knew, Verdi still had a desperate emotional attachment to what he saw as the only other survivor of his little family, his former father-in-law.

It was around this time that Verdi began to be seen by many Italians as an important nationalist. In later productions of *Ernani,* a scene when the new emperor, Carlo, is persuaded to give amnesty to the rebels reminded many in the audience of the new Pope Pius IX granting amnesty to pro-Italian/anti-Austrian revolutionaries who had been locked in dungeons for fifteen years. The audience cried out in appreciation, often changing the lyrics—"Pio Nono" (the Italian version of Pius IX's name) instead of "Carlo"—to suit the situation. Choruses from *Nabucco* and *I Lombard,* operas that by now had played all over Italy, also ignited a patriotic fervor. Often large groups of people would gather to sing the choruses, which made the Austrian authorities nervous.

Italians were beginning to tire of the Austrian yoke, and Verdi's operas presented situations that reminded the Italian people of their oppression. In response, Austrian authorities carefully monitored Verdi's librettos. A new social conscience was emerging, causing wealthy Italians to care more about the lot of the poor. Italians, feeling a consolidated pride, would look after other Italians. This united both classes in a hatred of Austrian rule and the negative conditions it engendered.

As there were no real patriotic heroes, Verdi almost inadvertently became a symbol of Italy's new attitude. Verdi believed—as virtually all of his fellow countrymen did—that Italians should rule Italy. Verdi, though, not only had no particular desire to be a symbol, he was no longer certain that he wanted to continue being a composer. He was still telling friends, including Muzio, that he wanted to retire from the theater, that he hated his career and every "accursed note." Much of this was a hysterical reaction to the pressure of success, his desire to please everyone and write scores for all the theaters that were clamoring to premiere one of his works. All the pressure only made him sicker. And the sicker he got the more disgusted he got with his career. In a sense, success came too early for Verdi. Although he would talk of his years of struggles, he was famous by his early twenties. He was under a constant, self-induced pressure to write a greater opera than the one before, one that would silence his critics and impress both audience and the press. As he entered his thirties, he continued writing.

His next work was *Macbeth*, an adaptation of the Shakespearean tragedy. Many of Verdi's peers thought he

Cover of *Macbeth*, the first of three Shakespearian plays Verdi adapted to opera *(Courtesy of Lebrecht Music and Arts)*

was foolish to do an adaptation of the play because Italian audiences were not very familiar with Shakespeare. It had been eight years since any of the bard's plays had even been produced in Italy, and that one, *Othello*, had not been well received. Italian opera composers, however, were attracted to Shakespeare's great stories, and Verdi, who had become knowledgeable of Shakespeare's work during his student years, was no exception.

Macbeth premiered at the Teatro della Pergola in Florence in March 1847. Verdi, now thirty-three, was determined to ensure that his show would receive the proper reception and took over the entire production. He rehearsed the singers, orchestra, and conductor incessantly. His focus was solely to get the production into a shape that would properly showcase his music. Most members of the company disliked Verdi because he didn't take the time out to pamper, encourage, or congratulate anyone when they got it right. He went so far as to insist on rehearsing one important sequence with the principal singers in the lobby just before the dress rehearsal, which had a specially invited audience. If *Macbeth* did not work, Verdi decided, it certainly would not be because of his music, so he was leaving nothing to chance.

Theatrical producers thought about special effects and other things that would amaze and delight the audience. A special trapdoor was built so that a ghost could rise out of the floor during the show. Verdi was convinced that if the effect was done right, people might rush to see the opera just to see the ghost. Whether it was the spectacle of ghosts and other effects, or simply appreciation for Verdi's music, *Macbeth* was a hit. There was much anticipation in Florence, which, like Naples, had both pro- and anti-Verdi factions. The box office was packed several hours before the performance. Although there were some naysayers, in general the work was received with applause and became a permanent fixture in the repertoire of major opera houses.

Some Italians, who had little knowledge of Shakespeare, saw *Macbeth* not as a drama but as a work of fantasy. They did not think Verdi's work compared favorably to other operatic works of that genre, such as Carl Maria von Weber's *Der Freischütz* (1821). These critics were in the minority, however, and many critics hailed Verdi's *Macbeth* as a work of power and sophistication. Verdi dedicated the opera to Antonio Barezzi.

Back in Milan, the political situation began simmering after the death of Cardinal Gaisruck, the archbishop, in November

1846. Since Gaisruck had been Austrian, Italian nationalists now demanded that the church name an Italian nobleman as his replacement. The church chose a man named Bartolomeo Romilli who would officially take the position in September of the following year. In the meantime authorities kept careful watch on theaters in case of outbreaks of civil unrest. During a performance of *Nabucco* at the Teatro Carcano, a political demonstration nearly erupted into violence. With rising prices and too many people out of work, Austrian authorities were on the lookout for anything that might smack of revolution. By September 1847, when Romilli became archbishop, Milan had reached a boiling point. Romilli's arrival ignited an outbreak known as the Lombard Revolt, which the police put down with extreme brutality. The Milanese quickly struck back against the police.

Verdi, meanwhile, was busy writing his next opera, *I masnadieri* (The Brigands). It is a tale of two brothers who love the same woman, and who become embroiled in conflict with their father and each other. It premiered in July 1847 at Her Majesty's Theatre in London. Verdi was exited over the prospect of a London premiere of his latest work, but fortune did not look kindly on *I masnadieri*. Although Verdi toned down some of the violently dramatic orchestral effects he usually went in for and wrote more arias than usual, the British public did not respond favorably to the work. They were also irked that there were more big moments for the tenor than for the popular soprano, Jenny Lind, who at the time was London's darling.

Adding to Verdi's upset was the fact that he hated London's hotels, food, and weather, and his inability to communicate intelligibly with the English-speaking people he encountered.

The Paris opera house staged many of Verdi's operas. *(Library of Congresss)*

Londoners were not the only audience to dislike Verdi's latest work—*I masnadieri* was seldom performed in Italy, either. On the brighter side, *I masnadieri* garnered Verdi the biggest commission he had received so far.

Verdi next went to Paris to work on a heavily revised version of *I Lombardi* for the Paris Opera. The new version would be called *Jerusalem* and would, in the style of French opera of the period, include a ballet. While in Paris, Verdi renewed his acquaintanceship with the soprano Giuseppina Strepponi. Strepponi had fallen on hard times due to problems with her voice. The major opera houses were no longer interested in her, and she had to advertise her services in the newspapers. When she did manage to get a job, she could barely get through the evening and received more jeers than applause. Although still in her thirties, Strepponi retired from performing and began a new life as a teacher in Paris. Verdi had known of her troubles, and had already sent her a letter expressing his love and devotion. They grew close, and he dedicated the score of *Jerusalem* to her.

Jerusalem, which premiered in November 1847, did not fare as well as *I Lombardi*. Even the Italian version, *Gerusalemm*, did not have nearly as much impact on the public as the original. But the Paris Opera paid Verdi as much money as if he had delivered a completely new work. Verdi raged that the singers, chorus, and orchestra at the Paris Opera where all substandard. Back in Italy he stipulated that if any theater producing *Gerusalemm* cut any music, aside from the ballet, they would have to pay a fine. Under any conditions *Gerusalemm* was not performed for very long.

Il corsaro (The Corsair) was another opera Verdi wrote for the detested publisher Francesco Lucca. Based on a poem by Lord Byron, it premiered in Trieste at the Teatro Grande in October 1848. Aside from writing a long letter of instructions to the soprano, he stayed away from Trieste and had nothing to do with the production. This was so atypical of the composer that it has been theorized that his disgust with Lucca had carried over to indifference toward the work. *Il corsaro* deals with the intrigue and bloodshed surrounding the corsair, or pirate, Corrado and his love for the harem-girl, Gulnara.

Around this time there were many changes in the political situation in Italy and throughout Europe. In 1848 there were student uprisings and revolutions in Hungary, Berlin, Vienna, and Paris, as well as Milan. Some of these were part of the general dissatisfaction of many European citizens who were

Political unrest across Europe influenced Verdi to include themes of patriotism and rebellion in his operas. *(Courtesy of The Granger Collection)*

downtrodden and resentful of the aristocracy. The Milanese felt oppressed by the Austrians. Milan was put under martial law in an attempt to control its citizenry. La Scala was closed because of protests over performances by the Austrian ballerina Fanny Elssler, and troops were called in to keep order. Verdi had stayed in Paris along with Strepponi since the premiere of *Jerusalem*, but was delighted to hear of the patriotic fervor of his fellow Italians.

Verdi was still in Paris during the infamous "*Cinque Giornate*" (Five Days), which occurred in Milan in March. This began when Austrian troops fired on a group of Milanese citizens gathering peacefully outside the Governor's Palace. Outraged by this incident, the citizens fought back against well-armed and highly trained soldiers with anything they could get their hands on—rocks, knives, bottles—and using a strategy of divide and conquer, managed to drive the Austrians out of the city. With the not-so-subtle patriotic subtext of his work, Verdi had helped to strike a chord of freedom-at-any-cost with his people. "Honour to these heroes! Honour to all of Italy," wrote Verdi, "which is now truly great!"

Things did not go smoothly, however. There were conflicts in the new Milanese government between the republicans, headed by one of the revolution's leaders, Giuseppe Mazzini, and the liberals (who were actually conservative). Mazzini wanted all of Italy to be one single republic, while the liberals preferred a monarchy, with Milan unified with a territory called the Piedmont. Unfortunately, the Austrians, who took back Milan and crushed the resistance, defeated Carlo Alberto, King of the Piedmont. Many of the Milanese citizens who had fought against the Austrians or aided the revolutionaries had to go into exile. These included Emanuele Muzio, Verdi's assistant. Muzio later made his way to Paris and was reunited with Verdi.

These events inspired Verdi to write the most politically charged opera of his career.

five

MANY
BATTLES

The city of Rome was undergoing its own rebellion when Verdi's *La battaglia di Legnano* (The Battle of Legnano) premiered there at the Teatro Argentina in January 1849. Its story concerned a love triangle, set against the background of the Lombards in Italy repelling the forces of the German emperor Frederick Barbarossa in the twelfth century. It did not take much imagination to realize that Verdi was really writing about the modern-day Milanese fighting off the hated, interloping Austrians.

Rome was particularly sympathetic to *La battaglia* because of the political upheaval in the city at the time, which was similar to the revolt in Milan. A Roman Council of Deputies established free elections in the city as Rome became a republic. As the citizens voted, there was singing and dancing in the streets.

Verdi had many admirers, and tickets to *La battaglia* were sold out within hours. The reaction from the citizens of Rome was delirious and sensational. A mob demanded

The score for Verdi's opera, *La battaglia*, incited rebellion among Italian patriots when it premiered in Rome. *(Courtesy of Lebrecht Music and Arts)*

to be let into the dress rehearsal and eventually broke into the theater. Squeezed together in the theater, the celebrants cheered Verdi as the opera progressed. On the night of the premiere, the audience insisted on the entire last act being repeated. The score for *La battaglia* seemed to become a battle hymn not only for Rome but for all of Italy.

The revolution and brief period of freedom in Rome was eventually quelled, though, and *La battaglia's* days were numbered. General Giuseppe Garibaldi, one of the leaders of the unification movement in Italy, was forced out of Rome and many of his young lieutenants were killed as the Austrians reoccupied the city. *La battaglia* managed to survive for a time in heavily censored and revised form under the title *L'assedio di Arlem*, but it was not able to regain the popularity it had when it debuted.

This cartoon shows Verdi being reprimanded by a censor. Although Verdi fought hard to keep his work in its original form, censors often edited or removed the more controversial aspects of Verdi's operas before they were staged. *(Courtesy of Lebrecht Music and Arts)*

Verdi planned to compose *Ferruccio*, another patriotic opera based on a novel by Francesco Domenico Guerrazzi. The novel's plot somewhat mirrored the political events in Italy. When the censors completely rejected the libretto, Verdi worked instead on *Luisa Miller*, which premiered in Naples in December 1849. The opera is a romantic melodrama about a tragic misunderstanding between the simple title heroine and the man she loves. He turns out to be the disguised son of the count that Luisa's father despises. There was almost as much drama behind the scenes as there was in the show. The Teatro San Carlo, which staged *Luisa Miller*, was so close to bankruptcy that it couldn't pay Verdi his fee when it was due. Verdi threatened to withdraw his score and leave the city. The management of the San Carlo, which, as usual, held onto Verdi's passport, vowed that they would never let him set foot out of Naples. Verdi countered that he would take up all copies of his score and seek political asylum on one of the French ships in the harbor. Things settled down when the San Carlo management promised Verdi that he would eventually be paid if he was patient.

Verdi eventually got his money, but the delay in payment created financial difficulties. Carlo Verdi helped his son out by selling his property in Roncole and giving him twenty-two hundred lire. Verdi had overextended himself by buying more property and a new farmhouse at Sant' Agata, in the countryside outside of Busseto. His parents eventually moved from Verdi's Palazzo Cavalli in Busseto to the new farmhouse where they settled in happily. He and his father jointly ran the farm at Sant' Agata, which brought in some profits.

The Verdis hoped that their busy and famous son would eventually return home and move in with them. They had his bed moved from the palazzo to the farmhouse at Sant' Agata. Carlo and his wife had no love for the city of Busseto, as Emanuele Muzio, whom they had befriended, had been told he would not be allowed to enter the competition for the post of *maestro di musica*. Verdi was appalled by all the petty minds and vendettas that were still operating in Busseto. In the meantime, he and Giuseppina Strepponi, both of whom had been based in Paris, decided to return to Italy for good.

Verdi spent some time with his parents at Sant' Agata while Strepponi went on to Parma. Then Verdi returned to his Palazzo Cavalli but was disheartened by the situation in Busseto with all its infighting. Verdi lived in part of the palazzo and rented out the ground floor to various shopkeepers. "This blessed, blessed, blessed Busseto!" he wrote in a sarcastic letter. "How beautiful! How elegant! What a place! What society! I am enthralled, and I don't know whether I can tear myself away from here soon."

To Verdi's chagrin, the town rejected Giuseppina Strepponi when she arrived in Busseto to join Verdi at his palazzo. Although she acted in many ways as Verdi's secretary and housekeeper, she was also known to be his mistress. Antonio Barezzi, Verdi's former father-in-law, was put in an awkward position because he didn't know what to say when people asked him if Strepponi was Verdi's wife. He himself wasn't certain. Strepponi's notoriety and her numerous affairs were well-known, even in Busseto. She was shunned by the pious citizens of the city, some of whom threw rocks at the palazzo. She was also sneered at in the street. Even when she became Verdi's wife, Strepponi retained her hatred of Busseto, which she damned as being devoid of culture and intellectual curiosity.

Verdi's opera *Stiffelio* premiered in Trieste in November 1850. Trieste was a conservative city with many Austrian sympathizers, but the Italian patriots of the underground were making their presence known. The censors were already wary of Verdi's nationalism, and were ready to take a hatchet to the libretto.

Verdi gave them plenty to censor. The plot of *Stiffelio* had to do with a Protestant minister whose wife is an adulteress. Worse, he forgives her for being unfaithful instead of casting her out, which was seen by some as an acceptance of immoral behavior. Religious rites were presented on stage; sacred music was performed; the minister sings from his pulpit. This was all too much. The authorities refused to let *Stiffelio* be performed unless it was so heavily revised it made little sense. *Stiffelio* was an abject failure. Verdi later revised it, but the original opera faded into obscurity.

Although Verdi was outraged at how the censorship of *Stiffelio* had completely ruined his work, he was not about to compromise his art for narrow minds. Others might have chosen only safe subjects to adapt into operas, works devoid of any controversial aspects. But composing an opera—writing music for all the instruments as well as vocal lines for several singers, and then arranging it while trying to be original and creative—was time-consuming work. Verdi needed to be inspired by his material. His aim was not to childishly shock, but to compose the greatest operas he possibly could. Verdi mulled over future projects, including an adaptation of Shakespeare's *King Lear*, which he thought about doing for many years but which never materialized. He also thought about having another premiere at La Scala, where his earliest operas had been produced. However, when he learned that they were staging some of his more recent works with what he considered to be severe cuts, he decided to offer his next work to La Fenice in Venice instead.

In Venice, Verdi had had another association, with a woman whom he always referred to in letters as "the angel." Her true identity was never known, but it was assumed that she had romantic feelings for Verdi that he may have shared. He first met her in 1844, and saw her occasionally over the years, though it is not known if they became intimate. Apparently the woman was comfortable enough to want to travel to

Busseto to visit Verdi, but Verdi headed her off. Even if there had been nothing between them, Verdi knew that Strepponi would have been suspicious. There were enough problems with Strepponi being in his palazzo without another woman adding to the turmoil.

Undaunted by scandal and conflict with the censors, his next opera was an adaptation of a play by Victor Hugo that had already caused a scandal in Paris, closing after one day. Verdi thought that Hugo's *Le Roi s'amuse* was "perhaps the greatest drama of modern times" with characters "worthy of Shakespeare . . . It is a subject that cannot fail . . . [We will] turn Venice upside down to make the censors permit this subject."

Hugo's drama presents a French monarch as a lecher who rapes Gilda, the daughter of his court jester, Triboulet. Triboulet is a hunchback and defames members of the court, saying they are bred from servants. *Le Roi s'amuse* was seen as dangerous in a period when people in Europe were beginning to rebel against the very idea of absolute monarchies. With a king as villain, and a hunchbacked court jester as hero, the play was immediately banned. Although Verdi's chief interest in the notorious play was its strong story and characters, the political aspects also appealed to him.

After his experiences with *Stiffelio*, however, Verdi could not help but have some concerns. The management of La Fenice assured Verdi that there would be no problems with an operatic version of Hugo's play. They even implied that they had the approval of the authorities—a blatant falsehood. They hoped that the librettist, Francesco Maria Piave, could smooth things over with the censors, but it would not be that easy. The censors did not demand revisions—they insisted that the opera could never be staged at all. Verdi was devastated. He had gone ahead and set much of the text to music in the belief that the libretto had been accepted. He completely rejected the idea of coming up with a brand new story line. It was either Hugo's play or it was nothing. He had written music not only to fit the text of the libretto, but which suited the atmosphere, situations, and characters. He could not simply reuse the music for another libretto. "My notes," wrote Verdi, ". . . are not written haphazardly . . . I always manage to give them a character all their own."

Piave and the director of La Fenice worked together to turn the libretto into something that would pass muster with the censors. The censors approved of this new version, but to Verdi all the guts and heart had been taken out of the story. He was baffled by many of the revisions, such as the removal of Triboulet's hunchback. He explained:

> I find it a very, very beautiful thing to portray this character who is deformed and ridiculous on the outside, and passionate and full of love inside. I chose this very subject just because of all these qualities, and these original traits [and] if they are taken out I cannot write the music for it. They have made an ordinary, commonplace, and cold thing out of an original, powerful drama.

Near the tragic end of the opera Triboulet is given a sack in which he thinks is the body of the man who raped his daughter Gilda. He doesn't realize that Gilda's body is in the sack until the final moments of the show; the gruesome discovery is meant to come as a horrible surprise. The censors objected to the woman's body being put in a sack. "If you take away the sack," Verdi ranted, "it is unlikely that Triboletto [Triboulet] would talk for half an hour to a corpse, without having a flash of lightning show him that it is his daughter."

Verdi told La Fenice that he would not allow the opera to be performed with the revised libretto. The season opened in a little more than two weeks, and the director of the opera house was desperate. Verdi had not finished the score and had stopped working on it. With Piave at his side, he importuned the director of public order to help him work out a compromise; there was yet another revision. Verdi agreed to this new version with some reluctance, but eventually was satisfied. With each revision, the work was given a new name. Finally it became *Rigoletto*, the title that stuck.

Rigoletto finally premiered in Venice in March 1851. It was an immediate success with the public, and the score was praised by critics. Nevertheless, there was hardly a review that did not comment upon the ugliness of the subject matter. That hardly stopped it from becoming one of Verdi's most popular operas.

As was often the case, Verdi's private life was tumultuous. As he was struggling to finish *Rigoletto* and literally losing sleep over the demands of the censors, he was embroiled in a serious conflict with his parents. The emotional upset over *Rigoletto*, which brought back Verdi's stomach problems, undoubtedly made the situation much worse.

Verdi was furious over the way the people of Busseto, including his own parents, treated Giuseppina Strepponi. Everyone seemed to ask them if they were married or not, and it was hard to determine which they would find worse: that Verdi was or was not married to such a notorious woman.

FIGURINI dell' Opera RIGOLETTO del Maestro G. VERDI

1851 costume designs for Verdi's opera, *Rigoletto* (*Courtesy of The Granger Collection*)

It particularly galled Verdi that his own father, Carlo, was one of the worst offenders. Verdi decided to cut off all relations with his parents.

He demanded that they vacate the farm at Sant' Agata so that he and Strepponi could move in and escape the narrow minds of Busseto. Verdi also decided that he and his father would no longer run the farm together. It was his intention to "separate himself in residence and in business" from his parents. Verdi even went so far as to have a notary draft a document of legal separation from the couple, who were now in their sixties.

Naturally, this did not sit well with his parents, and contact between them and their son was cut off. Carlo Verdi made scenes in Busseto, which only made his son angrier. Then there was a conflict over a chicken yard and its income, which his mother claimed rights to over Verdi's objections.

The Verdis were in terrible financial straits—the separation did not help—and their son wasn't doing much better. As they could not afford the rent on a little house where they hoped to move, Verdi lent them the money and then demanded they repay it almost immediately. Carlo was forced to borrow money from many of his friends in Busseto.

Although much is sheathed in mystery, it has been suggested that Verdi's split with his parents came about because Giuseppina Strepponi became pregnant. An infant named Santa Streppini, possibly Verdi's daughter, was dropped off at a home for abandoned babies in April 1851. Had Verdi acknowledged this child, by law he would have had to acknowledge all of Strepponi's other illegitimate children. It was common for the parents of illegitimate children to simply drop them off at foundling homes, where they would hopefully be eventually united with foster parents. This practice was considered deplorable, especially as it put the burden for the children's upkeep on an already overtaxed charity system. Once the child was entered into this system, there was no way for a famous individual such as Verdi to claim her without an ugly public uproar.

Verdi's mother was so upset over the estrangement that she became ill just as she and Carlo were leaving Sant' Agata. Undoubtedly Carlo blamed his wife's illness on Verdi. Even the townspeople who might have forgiven Verdi for living with Strepponi could not forgive his treatment of his parents. This was a society in which a man was judged by the regard he held for the people who had brought him into the world. Verdi's mentor and former father-in-law, Antonio Barezzi, refused to go to Venice to see *Rigoletto*, and gradually withdrew from the young man he'd once treated as a son.

Verdi and Strepponi were quite alone in Sant' Agata.

six
PRISONER
OF PARIS

When Giuseppe Verdi's mother died in July 1851, the emotional toll was almost too much for him to bear. His grief was intensified by his guilt over his estrangement from his parents. He spent his days mourning and being consoled by Strepponi. His former assistant Emanuele Muzio came to Sant' Agata and took care of all the funeral arrangements. A few months later when Carlo Verdi took ill, his son took it upon himself to take care of the lonely man.

In between, Verdi and Strepponi went to Paris for a respite from the isolation and tension in Sant' Agata and Busseto. Strepponi in particular was delighted to get away from the provincial people in Busseto. In Paris, she and Verdi went to the theater, where they saw the play *La Dame aux camelias* (Lady of the Camellias) by Alexander Dumas fils. During the day Verdi called on several impresarios with whom he held discussions on possible future productions.

This painting depicts a scene from Alexander Dumas fils's play, *La Dame aux Camélias*. Verdi later based his opera, *La traviata*, on this play. *(Courtesy of Lebrecht Music and Arts)*

While in Paris, Verdi defended Strepponi in a letter to Antonio Barezzi, whom he still addressed as his father-in-law:

Who knows what relationship exists between us? What business connections? What ties? What rights I have over her, and she over me? Who knows whether she is or is not my wife? And if she were, who knows what particular motives, what reasons we have for not making that public? Who knows whether it is good or bad? Why could it not also be good? And if it were bad, who has the right to hurl curses at us? But I will say that in my house people owe to her the same respect owed to me, or even greater respect, and that no one is allowed to fall short in that, for any reason whatever; that really she has every right to respect because of her behavior, her spirit, and because of the special concern she never fails to show for others.

In addition to the pain of his mother's death and his friends' rejection of the woman he loved—not to mention his health problems—Verdi also had to deal with what he saw as improper tactics employed by his longtime publisher, Ricordi. Verdi was angered that Ricordi expected him to honor his contracts on every point, no matter how disadvantageous to the composer. All of these problems, however, did not prevent Verdi from working on his next opera, *Il trovatore* (The Troubadour).

Il trovatore is the story of two brothers, Manrico and the Count di Luna, who grow up to become bitter enemies completely unaware of their true relationship. Manrico was kidnapped as a baby by the gypsy woman Azucena in revenge

Il trovatore quickly became one of Verdi's most popular operas. *(Courtesy of the Granger Collection)*

for her mother being burned at the stake for witchcraft. Although everyone believes that Azucena threw the baby into the same pyre, in her hysteria she accidentally threw her own baby into the flames. She has raised Manrico as a gypsy and rebel. Manrico and his brother, the count, are rivals for the hand of the beautiful Leonora. When the count captures Manrico and has him killed, Azucena triumphantly cries out that he has killed his own brother. Although she has grown to love Manrico as her own son, the conclusion makes clear that revenge is much more important to her.

Verdi wanted to experiment with this work by making it all of a piece. He would cut out all of the choruses, duets, and arias and write music that simply flowed from one scene to the next without interruption for individual numbers. The music would still be melodious and vocally interesting, but it would not be broken up into different types of songs. Eventually Verdi would compose this type of opera, but in the end *Il trovatore* remained traditional. Verdi wrote especially dramatic numbers that built upon all that he had learned from his previous works. The most famous number is the "Anvil Chorus" sung by the gypsies as they work.

The libretto for the opera was fashioned by Salvatore Cammarano, who became gravely ill and died before he could finish it. As he left behind a wife and six children, Verdi forwarded full payment for the libretto to the widow. The work was finished by a friend of Cammarano's, a poet named Leone Emanuele Bardare. There were also problems with casting, as Verdi was afraid the two women who sang Leonora and Azucena would have a battle of egos. Luckily their rivalry did not disrupt the performances. *Il trovatore* premiered in Rome in January 1853 and was an immediate success.

The delighted public took up Verdi's melodies and sang them in the streets. It quickly became the most popular of Verdi's operas so far.

Verdi's next opera, *La traviata* (The Fallen Woman), was based on the play *La Dame aux camelias* that he and Strepponi saw in Paris. It is hard not to imagine that Verdi saw in the play's heroine some similarities to his own beloved Strepponi. With *La traviata*, Verdi showed the world how a woman could be notorious, and yet have a good and noble heart.

The heroine of the story, Violetta, is an infamous courtesan (kept woman) who falls in love with the young and innocent Alfredo. The two go to live together, but Alfredo's father, Germont, tells Violetta that her relationship with Alfredo is having a negative effect on his family, and that he fears it will eventually cause the ruin of the young man. Germont also fears that his daughter will never be wed as long as her brother is living with Violetta. Violetta is moved by the father's words, and anxious not to hurt Alfredo or his family. Although deeply in love with Alfredo, she tells him that she is returning to her former lover. Deeply hurt, Alfredo heaps verbal abuse on her at a public gathering. Finally he learns the true reason that Violetta left him, and rushes to her side, only to find her sick with consumption (tuberculosis). They renew their vows of love, but Violetta dies.

La traviata premiered at La Fenice in Venice in March 1853. Verdi himself pronounced it a disaster. In later years many assumed the problem was in the casting of a rather large woman as Violetta, who was supposed to be wasting away due to illness. Although the soprano was not the perfect Violetta in physical size, her singing was heartily applauded and considered one of the best things in the performance. Similarly, it was supposed that the problem was that the setting was changed from the current period to around 1700, which the censors thought would be safer. But *La traviata* was presented as a period piece even after it finally became successful. The problem was that with the exception of Violetta, the singers were not up to the demands of the music, severely weakening the production's impact.

Verdi had longed feared weak singers would ruin his work. His music could put great demands on its singers. He often employed a bigger orchestra than the *bel canto* operas, with a much larger and louder sound. A "Verdi tenor" became known as a tenor who could handle the dramatic intensity of Verdi's music, hitting all the high notes, while still being heard above the orchestra.

As such, Verdi had been prepared for the singers to fail. At rehearsals he told the singers that their vocalizing was not adequate. He protested to the management of La Fenice that they be replaced, but they refused to comply. Luckily, the following year a revised version of the work was presented by another theater in Venice, the San Benedetto. With the right singers cast in the roles, the new *La traviata* became a smashing success. Verdi was both elated and vindicated. "Then it was a fiasco," he noted. "Now it is creating an uproar."

At forty, Verdi was famous enough for people to want to write his biography. He was approached by a publisher named Luzzati, who wanted to add the composer's life stories to his series of volumes about famous, successful people. Verdi agreed to draw up some biographical notes and to send them on to the publisher. His only stipulation was that certain things not be excised. These included his attacks on the

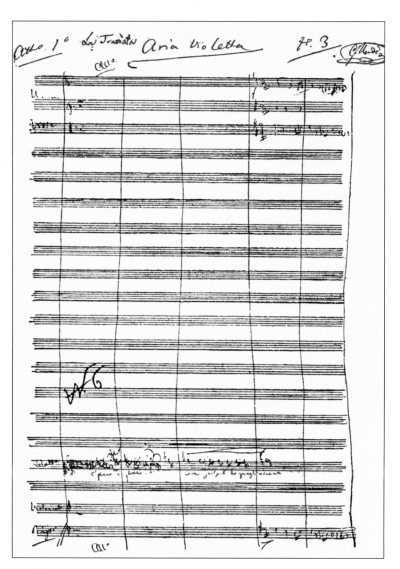

Page from the score of *La traviata* in Verdi's handwriting *(Courtesy of Lebrecht Music and Arts)*

priests who tried to prevent his appointment as music master in Busseto, and his praise of Antonio Barezzi. Despite the tensions caused by Strepponi's presence in his life, Verdi still loved and respected his former mentor and father-in-law.

A conflict between Verdi and the publisher erupted when Luzzati decided to edit the manuscript in a way that was not to Verdi's liking. Luzzati took offense that the busy Verdi used intermediaries to write to him. Luzzati bragged that all of Italy's "most famous people" wrote to him directly. Verdi took this comment as a slight, as if Luzzati were saying that Verdi was not in these people's league. Warned against presenting the manuscript as authorized by Verdi, Luzzati asked Verdi for damages. He expected the composer to make up whatever profits he might lose by not presenting an authorized biography. This infuriated the composer, who did everything he could to get the biography away from Luzzati.

"I never asked to be among Signor Luzzati's Elected Ones," wrote Verdi. "He asked me first . . . and was desperately insistent. Signor Luzzati does not know me either as a man or a composer. If he knew me, he would be convinced that I have little desire to be guided by him into the temple of immortality." Eventually Luzzati decided it would be wise to drop the project, and the biography was not completed or released.

In addition to composing, Verdi spent much time overseeing his farm at Sant' Agata. In his younger days he had spent virtually every minute composing but now made time for more relaxing activities. Although Verdi hired a foreman to run things, he looked after many aspects of the business himself. He sold pork from his slaughterhouse, bred and traded horses and cattle, and grew fruits and vegetables in his fields. There were stables, a nursery full of plants, and a beautifully landscaped garden. He was never afraid of trying something new, be it a new breed of horse or strain of grape. The men who managed the various aspects of his business had to write up weekly reports, which Verdi studied carefully. When he had the time, Verdi would inspect and investigate and write up the reports himself.

As he worked in the garden, Verdi mulled over his plans, never forgotten, to adapt *King Lear* for the operatic stage. He loved Shakespeare's story, and knew he could compose vivid music for each of the characters.

Instead Verdi composed *Les vêpres siciliennes/I vespri siciliani* (The Sicilian Vespers) for the Paris Opera, where it premiered in June 1855. Verdi was not happy at having to honor an old commitment to the Paris Opera for a number of reasons. First, he was angered at all the unauthorized cuts and changes made in his other operas that had played at the house. Second, he would have to compose to a French libretto, which would be much more difficult than crafting music for words in his native Italian. He complained that he could "have written two or three operas in Italian with more pleasure and greater financial return." At least he would be composing a libretto by the well-known librettist Augustin Eugène Scribe, whom he had specifically demanded. Scribe offered Verdi several ideas and librettos before Verdi decided upon the right one to set to music.

Les vêpres siciliennes takes place in Palermo in the thirteenth century when Sicily was under French rule. The heroine Helene plans to assassinate the hated French viceroy Guy de Montfort. Helene's lover, Henri, prevents the assassination when he discovers that Montfort is his father. Helene is arrested, but forgives Henri when she learns his motives. Montfort agrees to pardon Helene, and allow his son to marry her if Henri will publicly acknowledge him as his father. In the climax, Helene learns that her fellow Sicilians plan to massacre Montfort and the other Frenchmen, including Henri, during the wedding. This creates a maddening, grotesque moral dilemma for her. Should she betray her comrades or allow her own lover to be murdered? She desperately tries to stop the wedding but is unable to; the massacre takes place in the brutal conclusion.

Verdi had cast approval. He had mixed feelings when Sophie Cruvelli, his preferred soprano for the piece, simply disappeared without a word. As there could be no rehearsals without her, Verdi seized the opportunity to try and cancel his contract. All of Paris, and indeed Europe, was

Augustin Eugène Scribe
(Courtesy of Lebrecht Music and Arts)

wondering what had become of Cruvelli. Police searched everywhere for the woman in vain, but the Paris Opera refused to release Verdi from his obligations. This meant that Verdi would have to spend even more time in Paris, when all he wanted to do was return to Sant' Agata. *Les vêpres siciliennes* was turning more and more into a bothersome chore for the composer.

Finally Cruvelli turned up in Paris. She had been vacationing in the Côte d'Azur with the baron she would soon marry. One crisis was averted, but Verdi was still exasperated with the inefficient working methods of the Paris Opera. He found it impossible to accept that a production already in rehearsal would have a projected opening night that was nearly six months away. He found the members of the orchestra to be lazy and slow to learn, and deplored Cruvelli's and the other singers' blasé attitude toward their work. He worried that he would never be able to leave Paris and get back to his farm.

The money he was losing by spending so much time on just one production particularly galled Verdi. He was hardly poor: he owned land, a business, and he was the most successful composer in Italy. But he still had many expenses (he had to pay farm employees and his librettists, for instance), and the opera companies and publishers were slow in sending royalties. Considering all the hours he put in both composing and tending to his farm, he thought he should have accumulated much more money. Although he was certainly affluent by many people's standards, Verdi did not see himself as being wealthy.

At rehearsals Verdi showed his temper and anger. He heard people whispering negative remarks about the music, and some of the singers suggested that the material was not worthy of them. When some of the cast walked out of rehearsals for one appointment or another, Verdi would storm out of the opera house in a rage. The more he caused scenes—no matter how deserved—the more the singers and musicians resented him. There were also French composers who simply resented his presence in Paris. Camille Saint-Saëns sniped that Verdi should stick to writing operas about wars and leave the romance to the French.

The opening night of *Les vêpres siciliennes* occurred during the Universal Exhibition, or World's Fair, in Paris. Verdi had no idea how the audience might react. On one hand, the directors of the opera would fill the hall with as many friends and Verdi supporters as possible. But there was also a large contingent who hated Verdi and made a vulgar pun out of his name that referred to fecal matter. Some Parisians thought that a work by a French composer should have been chosen for the Exhibition. But Verdi was one of the biggest and most important people in opera and getting him was seen as a coup. He stirred up controversy and interest. Verdi knew that it could go either way.

As it turned out, *Les vêpres siciliennes* was well received by the audience. French composer Hector Berlioz commented that it was a work of lasting grandeur and Verdi's greatest achievement by far. But the opera did not stay in the repertoire for long. Back in Italy, the authorities would have censored it out of existence. The plot smacked too much of the current political situation and even a suggestion of assassination was forbidden. This prompted Verdi to come up with an alternate Italian version that he called *Giovanna de Guzman*, but this was not as successful.

Many years later the opera gained a new life as *I vespri siciliani*. Some modern-day critics find the work under any name self-conscious and suggest that Verdi was too influenced by the epic operas of Giacomo Meyerbeer. Generally working from librettos by Scribe, Meyerbeer had almost single-handedly created the genre of flamboyant, larger-than-life nineteenth-century French Grand Opera. His style was quite different from Verdi's, but Verdi admired Meyerbeer more than any other contemporary composer. *Les vêpres siciliennes* was Verdi's attempt to experiment with new forms and approaches without going too far from what made his own music unique.

Back home in Italy, Verdi found himself embroiled in old conflicts. Although Emanuele Muzio remained his good friend and sometime assistant, Muzio had embarked on his own operatic career with no great success. While a couple of his works had been produced, they did not earn him enough to compose full time. Again it was suggested that he become the *maestro di cappella* at a church in Busseto and also run the Philharmonic Society. Verdi readily agreed to give Muzio his backing and was certain he would get the post.

But certain forces—those who did not care for Verdi and did not wish to support his protégé—seemed determined to undermine Muzio's chances. He was told that he would have to give up all operatic ambitions if he were given the post. The salary would be substandard. Worse, he was told he would have to compete for the post in a contest just as Verdi had. Muzio found this humiliating, especially as the Great Giuseppe Verdi was going to vouch for him. In the end, he was not awarded the post.

Verdi was livid. In a letter to the Philharmonic Society he wrote:

> In any other place, in any matter relating to music, I would have been able to get what you and I wished: in any other town, I would have had the support of the civil and ecclesiastic authorities: in my own town, it was not possible. Perhaps in other places people have a bit of esteem and respect for my name. That's all right: that is perfectly right, nor am I complaining about it. . . . In some other place, I repeat, I would have succeeded; in Busseto (it is laughable) I could not.

seven

THE FORCE OF DESTINY

Verdi had become increasingly disenchanted with his publisher Ricordi, and things finally came to a boil in late 1855. Verdi claimed that Ricordi had no respect for him as a man or a composer. He said the scores of his works that Ricordi's company issued were loaded with careless errors, which led to sloppy productions. He accused the publisher of being so anxious to profit off of him that they sold the rights for his operas to companies that were not capable of first-class productions. If a production was poor it not only damaged his reputation, he argued, but robbed him of royalties. Once word of mouth got around about a production's poor quality, people would not pay for tickets. He complained that he had to run around overseeing many of these productions in order to improve them—and at his own expense.

Verdi went so far as to travel to England to put a halt to productions employing pirated editions of his scores. England would only pay royalties to foreign composers whose countries had a special treaty with the British government.

This did not include Italy. It was suggested to Verdi that he change his citizenship to French so he could collect British royalties, which would have been significant. "I want to remain what I am," he said, "a peasant from Roncole."

Verdi was hardly a peasant any longer. In 1856, he spent 300,000 francs to buy a large piece of property collectively known as Piantadoro. Northeast of Sant' Agata, it consisted of several farms. The acquisition of this property made Verdi a major landowner in the area. The worth of the property increased as Verdi rebuilt the farmhouses and made other improvements to the land.

Emanuele Muzio arranged for Ricordi to come to Sant' Agata so that he and Verdi could come to some terms. Ricordi was anxious to mend fences with the composer. If Verdi had taken his work to another publishing house, it might have meant financial ruin for Ricordi. Therefore, Ricordi was careful not to inflame his greatest asset, the prickly Verdi. The two men reached a temporary agreement and truce.

Verdi's next project was *Simon Boccanegra,* the story of a man in fourteenth-century Genoa who is involved in murderous intrigue surrounding his daughter and her grandfather. Verdi's stomach troubled him terribly as he hastened to finish the score. The show premiered at La Fenice in Venice in March 1857. The opening night did not go well and things improved only slightly with future performances. Anti-Verdi factions were blamed, as well as what was considered an impenetrable libretto by Francesco Maria Piave. When Verdi heard a rumor that Piave had credited the composer with the libretto, Verdi blasted the man, who gave him a hurt denial. *Simon Boccanegra* did not find any kind of success until Verdi revised it several years later.

This scene depicts an 1861 production of Verdi's *Un ballo in maschera.*
(Courtesy of Lebrecht Music and Arts)

Verdi signed a contract for a brand-new opera for the San Carlo in Naples. He hoped to finally realize his ambition to set *King Lear* to music. He even engaged the services of the poet Antonio Somma to fashion a libretto, which Verdi approved. But for a variety of reasons—primarily the singers the San Carlo planned to use—this plan was scrapped and a completely different libretto was substituted. Verdi began work on *Un ballo in maschera* (The Masked Ball). *Un ballo in maschera* was loosely based on the assassination of Gustav III of Sweden, who was stabbed to death during a royal masked ball. Right away there were problems with the Neapolitan censors, who wanted changes made to the characters, the plot, and the settings. Even after the libretto was heavily revised, a new problem arose when French emperor Napoleon III was nearly assassinated. The censors then chose their own Neapolitan poet to rewrite the libretto yet again, and expected Verdi to come through with the score despite his objections. Verdi would have nothing to do with the new libretto and tried to break his contract with the San Carlo. Despite the fact that Verdi was now the most famous, successful, and admired composer in Italy, the censor ordered the composer's arrest. The San Carlo was told to sue him for damages as well.

Verdi fought back by filing his own lawsuit against the San Carlo. His lawyer prepared a defense for Verdi in which it was stated that the play upon which *Un ballo's* libretto had been based was currently playing in Rome without any problem from the censors. Verdi was allowed to take the original libretto and flee Naples. The lawsuit and counter suit were settled out of court.

The Teatro Apollo in Rome agreed to stage *Un ballo in maschera*. The censors demanded two changes, however. The king who is assassinated had to be turned into a lesser personage, perhaps a count. They also insisted that the story not take place in Europe at all. The so-called American version of the opera takes place in Boston, where the governor is murdered at the ball. In later decades the setting was changed to Sweden.

To accommodate the censors, the king was changed to Riccardo, count of Warwick and governor of Boston. Riccardo has fallen in love with Amelia, the wife of his aide and close friend, Renato. When Renato discovers this betrayal, he is full of rage and despair. After threatening his wife with death, he joins some conspirators who plan to murder Riccardo at the ball. Renato stabs his friend; as he dies, Riccardo tells Renato that his relationship with Amelia was entirely chaste. To spare Renato pain, they had planned to separate and never see one another again. Renato and the entire company grieve over the fallen Riccardo.

Un ballo in maschera finally premiered in Rome in February 1859. It would be unusual for an opera by Verdi to open without some problem with the cast and *Un ballo* was no exception. Verdi was irritated when the lead soprano asked him to help her learn her role. He replied that she should have memorized the score completely before daring to show up for rehearsal. Strepponi, who knew the woman from her own singing days, interceded and things moved smoothly after that.

Un ballo in maschera is considered one of Verdi's finest scores, and perhaps the one in which the music most directly reflects the emotions of the characters. The work includes unusual choruses—such as one based on the cadences of laughter. It was an immediate and tremendous success.

While Verdi enjoyed *Un ballo in maschera*'s success, the political situation in Italy was becoming precarious. A nationalistic army was being formed in the Piedmont territory, also known as the Kingdom of Sardinia. In reaction, Austria sent ten thousand troops into the strategically located city of Piacenza. The police commissioner was replaced with a man nicknamed "The Killer." Landowners were told to turn over virtually everything of value, and people in town were ordered to take Austrian soldiers in as free boarders—or else. Many Italian loyalists left Piacenza to join the army in Piedmont. Meanwhile, Austrian officers were told to evacuate their families in case of an uprising, although political demonstrations in the city were put down just as quickly as they were started.

Austria ordered Piedmont to disband its army. Count Camillo Benso di Cavour, President of the Council of State in Piedmont, responded that the Austrians should leave Piacenza before they could expect that to happen. The Austrians essentially replied that if the Italians wanted the city, the Italians would have to take it back by force. Both Italian and Austrian forces gathered in Piacenza, and fighting soon broke out. Piacenza was in a state of siege. It was later reported that Cavour opened his window and began singing a triumphant aria from *Il trovatore*.

Verdi had been advised to leave Sant' Agata, as it was only about twenty-five miles from the fighting. Verdi did not want to leave, however. The French forces of Napoleon III joined the Piedmont Army and managed early victories against the Austrians, even as the latter invaded the Piedmont. The fighting

A nationalistic Italian army, fighting with the help of French soldiers, managed to expel the Austrian military from the Piedmont region in 1859. *(Courtesy of Mary Evans Picture Library)*

Villa at Sant' Agata, Verdi's country home

in Piacenza devastated the city but eventually the Franco-Piedmont Army routed the Austrians. As a final sally, the retreating Austrian troops dynamited everything that still stood. But the citizens of Piacenza were finally free.

Verdi had not been pleased that his poor health made him a mere distant observer of the war instead of a participant. "But what can I do," he wrote "who am not able to complete a three-mile march, who cannot stand five minutes of sun on my head, and a little wind or humidity gives me sore throats that send me to bed, sometimes for weeks? What a miserable nature I have! Good for nothing!"

Knowing the awful cost of the war in human lives, Verdi decided to appeal to his fellow Italians for money to help the families of dead and wounded soldiers. He contributed

Giuseppina Strepponi presented this autographed portrait of herself to Verdi on his sixty-fifth birthday. *(Courtesy of Lebrecht Music and Art)*

550 francs to a fund set up for this purpose, and urged others to contribute. Many of the farmers in the area, as well as members of the Barezzi family, gave money to the fund. Whatever harsh feelings the people who lived in Busseto may have had for Verdi and Strepponi, they did not allow that to stop them from sending in contributions for such an important cause.

The brief joy at the liberation of Piacenza was ended when details slipped out regarding the Treaty of Villafranca signed by Italy and Austria. Verdi was dismayed to learn that Austria would still hold on to such important Italian cities as Venice. Italy as a nation was still not free. Verdi was thankful that he had declined to write the national hymn that the mayor of Milan had requested from him. It was not yet the time for such a hymn, as Italy was far from being unified. The next step was for various cities to become annexed to the Piedmont.

On August 29, 1859, Verdi and Giuseppina Strepponi finally got married in a village outside Geneva. Besides the couple and the priest, there were two witnesses: the bell

In 1859, many Italians supported Verdi in his efforts to unify Italy.
(Courtesy of Lebrecht Music and Arts)

ringer of the church and the driver of their coach. As Verdi
had never thought it was anyone's business whether or not he
and Strepponi were married, he did not tell or invite anyone
to the wedding, nor was there any kind of celebration. Back
in Busseto, Verdi was chosen to represent the city as a deputy
to the Assembly of the Parma Provinces. The assembly was
for the purposes of promoting annexation and a free Italy.
Eventually this led to the formation of the Royal Provinces
of Emilia (formerly the Parma Provinces). Verdi was flattered
to be chosen and determined to unify as much of Italy as
possible with the Piedmont and get out from under Austrian
rule. Italy was in a state of confusing flux and turmoil, a
divided land with different sovereigns and laws and frequent
displays of civil unrest. In unification and independence,
Verdi said, "rests the future greatness and regeneration of
our native land."

Verdi, now in his late forties, had toyed with the idea of

retirement for some time. He told journalists in 1859 that he was definitely and absolutely finished with composing. He had all the money he needed now, and enjoyed his quiet life with his wife at the farm at Sant' Agata. The turmoil and irritation he endured trying to have one of his operas correctly produced wreaked havoc on his emotional and physical health. He said he was *through* and he meant it.

Meanwhile, Italy was going through many changes on the political front. Throughout the early 1860s General Giuseppe Garibaldi became firmly entrenched as the leader of the movement to unify Italy. Beginning initially with a ragtag group of rebels, Garibaldi managed to build up a formidable army. He succeeded in not only tearing some cities out of the hands of Austrians, but also in taking over other Italian cities, such as Naples, that wished to secede (or divide themselves) from the rest of the country. This eventually resulted in the formation of the Kingdom of Italy.

Verdi was importuned to become a deputy to the first parliament of the new kingdom. Verdi was a patriot, but he did not consider himself to be a politician.

> I have not campaigned. I will not campaign, nor will I take a step to insure my election. I will serve, although at a heavy sacrifice to myself, if I am elected; and you know the reasons why I must do so. Nevertheless I am resolved to resign as soon as I can.

Verdi was not thrilled when he was elected by a narrow margin.

Just as he was elected deputy to the parliament, Verdi became interested in composing again. An offer of a commission from the Imperial Theatre of St. Petersburg in Russia intrigued him. Even outside of Italy Verdi had to deal with censors, and his first suggestion for the commission was flatly turned down. His second suggestion resulted in *La forza del destino* (The Force of Destiny), which premiered in November 1862.

In *La Forza del destino*, the lead female character, Leonora, has fallen in love with a man, Alvaro, of whom her father, a Spanish marchese, disapproves. During an argument between the two men, Alvaro throws his pistol at the marchese's feet to indicate surrender. Unfortunately, the gun goes off, killing the marchese. The rest of the story details the convoluted and fascinating fates of Leonora and Alvaro as the lovers are pursued by Carlo, Leonora's vengeful brother. At one point the two men, in disguise, even become friends. But it ends in tragedy, with Carlo killing his sister and Alvaro committing suicide. As the 1862 audience found this all too depressing, the libretto was later revised to have Alvaro left alive at the end.

The production had to be postponed for several months because of the illness of the lead soprano. Verdi would not allow a performance to go on with a lesser singer in the role. Although the work was well received in St. Petersburg, Verdi always had nagging doubts about it. There was one production of the opera in Rome under the title *Don Alvaro*, but otherwise it did not play in Italy for several years. However, Verdi allowed it to be performed in other countries during this period.

With *La forza del destino* Verdi was still attempting to pull away from the traditional approach of the number operas. Critics noted that because the opera dealt with a specific

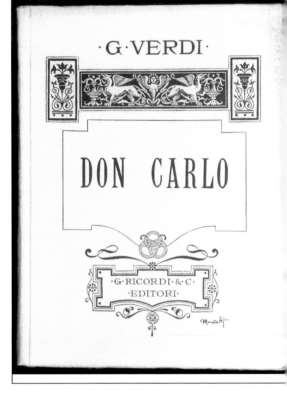

Don Carlo gained critical acclaim despite not being well received by the public. *(Courtesy of Lebrecht Music and Arts)*

idea—the randomness of life and nature—the music has a very loose, sprawling approach. This was in marked contrast to the tight, concise nature of earlier Verdi works. *La forza del destino* was also one of Verdi's longest operas. Composing *La forza del destino* had fired up Verdi's artistic juices and he banished all thoughts of retirement from his mind. Despite the postponement, things had gone so well in St. Petersburg that Verdi thought he might try his hand at the Paris Opera once again. Originally he was offered a libretto that had been written for the now dead Giacomo Meyerbeer, but he refused. The Opera then offered him a second libretto, which he accepted. This became *Don Carlo*.

Don Carlo (sometimes known as *Don Carlos*) is the story of massive political forces of the sixteenth century conspiring against the love of Carlos, the son of King Philip of Spain, for the Frenchwoman Elisabeth. Although Elisabeth was supposed to have married Carlos, it is decided that she marry Philip instead for political purposes. The heartache of the young lovers underlies another long, sprawling story of court intrigue and betrayal. *Don Carlo* was even longer than *La forza del destino*. Right away cuts had to be made so that opera goers could catch the last trains home. At one time there were no less than eight official versions of the score. When sung in French the opera is generally five acts, while the Italian version has only four. Although critics declared that *Don Carlo* contained some of Verdi's most brilliant music, the work never quite caught on with the public. Even the Paris Opera failed to stage it again after its premiere and follow-up performances in March 1867.

Verdi found the Paris Opera just as sloppy as ever. He believed the musicians and singers were lazy and required too many hours of rehearsal. Everyone seemed to have an opinion about the music and the story, no matter how ill informed. Verdi tried to keep calm, but it wasn't easy. As Verdi wrote a friend, "It was not a success! I don't know what the future may hold, but I shouldn't be surprised if things were to change." During the rehearsals for *Don Carlo*, Verdi's father had taken ill and died in 1866 at the age of eighty-two. For days after, Verdi could not attend rehearsals or coach the singers. Verdi also worried about his aged aunt, who'd been living with his father, and her seven-year-old granddaughter. He had the two of them moved to Sant' Agata, where servants would be able to look after them. "You can just imagine whether I, who have so little faith in anything," he wrote, "can have any in the reliability of two servants [who are] now practically masters in my house."

A few months later, his former father-in-law and mentor, Antonio Barezzi, also passed away at age seventy-nine. Verdi and Strepponi were at his bedside on the day he died. Verdi went to the piano and played Barezzi's favorite of all his compositions, the "Va, pensiero" chorus from *Nabucco*. The story goes that Barezzi died as he listened to this music, raising his hand and saying *"Mio Verdi* [My Verdi]."

"You know," Verdi wrote of Barezzi, "that I owe him everything, everything, everything."

eight
THE GENIUS OF TWILIGHT

I taly was slowly changing. The aristocratic class with its privileged way of life was beginning to die out. As a population boom hit Italy, the middle class filled the cities to bursting. Following the lead of Paris, Italy built sewage systems and new buildings to supply the demand for housing. In the 1870s gas would replace candles, making it possible for the first time to dim house lights in theaters. Verdi observed all these changes with mixed emotions. One thing remained constant: he was an artist and an artist created. Some of Verdi's finest work lay ahead. But he still insisted to everyone that he was retired.

On the farm at Sant'Agata Verdi would get up at dawn and work in his fields until he was too tired to move. There were days when he hardly said a word to his wife. The composer was frequently in bad form and grumpy. Strepponi endured loneliness and isolation on the farm. To please her, Verdi bought a second residence in Genoa, where they frequently spent the winter months. There the two would play billiards as Verdi grumbled about one thing or another. He would also play the piano and act as a handyman, fixing broken locks and jammed doors. Verdi hated the cook that his wife had hired but in general the couple was happy.

In August 1868, it was time for the grand opening of the Teatro Verdi, the opera house built in Busseto. Verdi was still not pleased with the alleged honor. Nevertheless he had given 10,000 lire to the construction fund. This was not an actual donation, however. Years before, he had advanced the town the money to fix a bridge on a road just outside town. When it looked like the town was going to renege on the debt, Verdi had put a chain across the bridge and allowed no one to use it. Now he forgave the debt as his contribution to the opera house.

Verdi doubted that Busseto could really afford to build or maintain the theater, and suspected it was named after him only to secure his financial participation. "This is more than an inconvenience," he railed, "it is an insult. . . . It was as if to say: 'Why should we consult him? He'll do it . . . he'll have to do it.' What right have they to do this?" Verdi hated that he had not been consulted about the project and even more loathed the idea that some of the townspeople who had caused him so much torment over the years believed they had contributed to his success. In his opinion, all the town did was give him a stipend thirty-two years previously that amounted to around 1200 francs. "I have carried your name with honor into all parts of the world. That is well worth 1200 francs."

Verdi may have been disturbed by the brouhaha over the opera house, but he was devastated by a friend's report from Milan. Verdi was told that the graves of his first wife Margherita

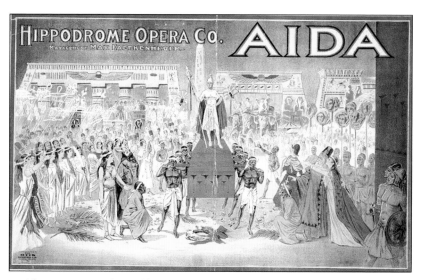

After immersing himself in Egyptian history and music, Verdi composed the score to *Aida*, which premiered in Cairo, Egypt. *(Library of Congress)*

and his son Icilio had been opened and their bones placed in a common burial mound. The same thing had probably happened to the remains of his daughter, Virginia, who had been buried in Bussetto. Verdi kept a copper box upon which he had written "Mementoes of my poor family." Inside the box were wedding rings and other jewelry.

In February 1869, a revised version of *La forza del destino* opened at La Scala, ending the long standing rift between the composer and the theater. (Many of Verdi's operas played the house but Verdi himself had not participated.) Although *La forza* was not a new work, very few members of the audience had heard it. Verdi conducted the rehearsals, oversaw the staging, and even helped pick out the costumes for the cast. He was impressed by the professionalism of the orchestra and soloists at La Scala, finding the theater much improved since the early days. The people at La Scala seemed especially splendid in comparison to those at the Paris Opera. Remembering his dreadful experiences with the French company, he resisted all entreaties to write a new opera for them.

However, he found he could not resist when he was offered a new commission from an unexpected source. *Aida* was conceived for a new opera house in Cairo, Egypt. The opera house had been opened during a celebration for the opening of the Suez Canal; its first production had been Verdi's *Rigoletto*. Verdi was asked to write a new opera for the house, and he agreed. He immersed himself in Egyptian history and music for weeks as he researched the locale and period and prepared to compose the score.

Aida is the story of the doomed love affair between Radames, a young heroic captain in the Egyptian Army, and Aida, an Ethiopian princess who has been enslaved by the Egyptians. Radames is also loved by another woman named Amneris. Aida is torn between her loyalty to her people and her father, the Ethiopian king, and her love for their enemy Radames. Arrested for treason, Radames is placed in an underground tomb to suffocate. He is glad, at least, that his beloved Aida can live out her life. To his dismay he discovers that she has hidden herself in the tomb—she does not want to live without him. The two die together as Amneris cries over Radames' tragic fate.

Aida premiered in Cairo in December 1871. Radames' love song, "Celeste Aida," and the "Triumphal March," as the Egyptian Army returns to the city, were especially well received. Although there were many larger-than-life crowd scenes and choruses, there was also a focus on individual characters. Therefore the opera was seen as a splendid combination of the Italian romantic tradition and French grand

German composer Richard Wagner heavily influenced opera-writing in the latter nineteenth century. Although Verdi respected Wagner as an artist, he did not appreciate Wagner's style or influence over Italian opera.

opera. *Aida* rapidly swept the world and became Verdi's most popular opera.

By this time the music of Richard Wagner, a famous German composer born the same year as Verdi, was finally being heard in Italy after being performed elsewhere for many years. Verdi attended a production of Wagner's *Lohengrin* and had a mixed reaction. "Much *verve* but without delicacy or poetry," wrote Verdi in his notes. Eventually fans

Verdi *(right)* and Arrigo Boito work together in Verdi's workroom.
(Courtesy of Lebrecht Music and Arts)

around the world divided themselves into pro-Wagner and pro-Verdi factions.

Verdi next decided to do a heavily revised version of *Simon Boccanegra* upon his publisher Ricordi's suggestion. His choice of librettist, Arrigo Boito, may have seemed surprising. Verdi had first met Boito when he attended a dinner to honor the composer Franco Faccio in the summer of 1863. Faccio's first opera had just been produced at La Scala. Boito, who was a young composer and writer, rose at one point to recite a poem as a toast to Italian art. "Here's to the health of Italian Art. May it soon escape, young and healthy, from the encircling limitations of the old and idiotic ways." He went on to suggest that the altar of Italian art had been stained and defamed.

When this poem was published, everyone saw it not only as a tribute to Faccio (the young and new), but as a rebuke and insult to Verdi (the old). Faccio was so horrified that he immediately sent a note of apology to Verdi. Faccio stayed in Verdi's good graces and conducted the Italian premiere of *Aida* at La Scala. Regardless of what Boito intended by his remarks, it was Verdi who remained at the forefront of Italian operatic art. Faccio's opera completely disappeared from the repertoire and in a few years Boito would, incredibly, find himself working not with Faccio but with Verdi.

Boito would make more of a mark as Verdi's librettist than as a composer. His *Mefistofele*, which premiered in 1868, did enter the repertoire, but he died before completing his second work, *Nerone*.

Boito and Verdi had settled their differences by the time they began to work together. Verdi's publisher Ricordi had done his best to heal the rift between the two. Aside from one new scene, Boito's work on the original libretto of *Simon Boccanegra* was to make many slight adjustments to the text. Verdi, however, made many changes to his score, including revisions to scenes that Boito had not changed at all. This second version of the work became the official version.

Many years went by before Verdi composed another opera. Even though Richard Wagner was now dead, Verdi found Italian musicians—students, teachers, and professionals—infected with what he called Germanism. He saw a sad state of decline in Italian music and opera in general. In 1882, Italy formed a Triple Alliance with Germany and its former oppressor and enemy, Austria. Verdi had always adored Paris, but now Berlin was considered both the capital and the cultural center of Europe. All of Italy seemed addicted to all things German. Verdi had difficulty adjusting to this state of affairs.

Verdi wrote: "Our music is different from German music, whose symphonies can survive in large halls, and quartets in small rooms. Our music, I say, has its seat principally in the theatre. Now the theatres without government aid can not exist. It is a fact no one can deny. They must all soon close and if one can hang on to life, it is an exception. La Scala, even La Scala, perhaps will close next year." Verdi eventually worked through this siege of melancholia by working on the score for *Otello*, an operatic adaptation of Shakespeare's *Othello*. The librettist for this was Arrigo Boito, who by now had become good friends with Verdi. This friendship was tested, however, when Verdi read a newspaper interview with Boito in which the latter said that he wished he could set the libretto to music himself. Angry, Verdi wrote to Boito and offered him the libretto. Boito explained that he had been misquoted and a placated Verdi continued working on the score.

Having been burned by opera companies in the past, Verdi decided to take no chances. His contract with La Scala gave him the right to cancel performances even after the final dress rehearsal if any element of the production wasn't up to his high standards. Absolutely no one could be admitted to rehearsals without his permission. One story claims that when the tenor playing Othello didn't stab himself with sufficient verve, Verdi grabbed the prop knife and enacted the scene himself, rolling down several steps onto the floor of the stage.

Otello is the tragic story of the Moor known as Othello, the governor of the island of Cyprus in the fifteenth century. His ensign, the malevolent Iago, convinces Othello that his

CHOCOLAT POULAIN

GOÛTEZ
ET
COMPAREZ
4 QUALITÉ
SANS RIVALE.

2me ACTE _ HOMMAGES A DESDEMONA.

This illustration depicts a scene from the second act of Verdi's *Otello*.
(Courtesy of Lebrecht Music and Arts)

beloved wife Desdemona is having an affair with a young of-
ficer named Cassio. Despite her desperate denials, a savagely
jealous Othello smothers Desdemona in their bedchamber.
After Iago's lies are exposed, the heartbroken Othello stabs
himself with a dagger.

Otello premiered in February 1887 in Milan. As it was
the first opera from Verdi in sixteen years, there was much
excitement and anticipation surrounding the premiere. *Otello*
was a triumph for the seventy-three-year-old composer. Early
in the morning crowds gathered outside Verdi's hotel to cheer
him. While Verdi was delighted with the public and critical
reaction, there came an inevitable letdown after the opening. Verdi told his friends, including Boito and Faccio, that
this would be his last hurrah. If he were younger he might
compose another opera, but now it was too late.

In Milan, Verdi founded Casa Verdi, a retirement home for musicians.

Verdi was alarmed at the reports of poverty and hunger in his country, especially in Southern Italy. He did not see the situation as improving any time soon. He did his part to try to help those less fortunate than himself. In Sant' Agata he built a small hospital for local people that still exists. He also founded a rest home for old and indigent musicians in Milan, which was built on property he had acquired for that purpose. This rest home also still exists and is popularly known as the Casa Verdi (House of Verdi). It houses more than a hundred musicians and is supported by royalties from Verdi's many productions.

Around this time, Verdi decided to compose one final opera. It was another Shakespearean adaptation, entitled *Falstaff*. This was not based on any one play but on a character named Falstaff who appears in *The Merry Wives of Windsor* and *Henry IV*. Falstaff is a portly, aging con-artist who hatches a scheme to acquire some money. The unlikely lover will seduce the wives of two rich men and therefore get at their husbands' fortunes. Receiving love letters from Falstaff, the two women hatch their own plan to teach the man a lesson. Falstaff is humiliated in the end, but happily leads everyone in a chorus to celebrate the absurdity of human nature.

Verdi had not composed a comic opera since *Un giorno di regno*, which he worked on right after the deaths of his first wife and children. That show had been his first dismal failure. As Verdi was back in a somewhat melancholic state, his friends worried that it would have an adverse effect on the score. As with *Otello*, however, Verdi's spirits began to rise the more he worked on the opera. Although there were difficult moments when he had to set the score aside, Verdi found it a joy to come up with music for *Falstaff*. His librettist was again Arrigo Boito. Much of Verdi's enthusiasm had to do with the fact that he completely trusted Boito and found his work to be superlative. Verdi cherished young Boito's friendship and encouragement.

Falstaff premiered at La Scala in February 1893. Verdi was seventy-nine. As with *Otello* there was much excitement over the new opera, but not as much suspense. With *Otello*, the public did not know if Verdi would still have his musical powers after such a long absence from the theater, but this was not the case with *Falstaff*. Everyone expected the work to be a masterpiece. While it was warmly received, the public and critics were also a bit put off by it.

With *Falstaff*, even more than *Otello*, Verdi had finally realized his ambition of composing a kind of musical drama that eliminated all arias and other set numbers. One cannot point to the score of *Falstaff* and pick out any outstanding songs or choruses. The melodies are very short, moving on to another theme before the audience can quite take hold of any one in particular. This is why *Falstaff* didn't quite catch on with the public like *Aida* or *La traviata*. The public enjoyed the opera but were a little baffled. After awhile this kind of opera, almost like a film score backing up the action on stage, would become the norm instead of the exception. The number opera was on its way out, although it would take some years for this to happen.

While working on *Falstaff*, Verdi became greatly distressed by the fate of his dear friend, Emanuele Muzio, who had been his pupil, assistant, and confidante for so many years. After the failure of his career as a composer, Muzio had gone to America and married. Muzio and his wife then moved to Paris, where their only child died and the marriage fell apart. Unable to find work as a conductor, Muzio gave singing lessons. He died alone in a Paris hospital in 1890. The great success achieved by Verdi had, sadly, eluded his dear friend. More losses followed. In 1897, Strepponi developed a lingering case of bronchitis. Bedridden for several weeks with a wracking cough and fever, she was eventually diagnosed with pneumonia. Verdi and his wife had planned to leave for Genoa to spend the winter, but Strepponi was too ill to go. She had no appetite and began wasting away. On November 14, 1897, she died. Verdi was disconsolate.

"Great grief does not demand great expression," he wrote a friend. "It asks for silence, isolation. I would even say the torture of reflection." Verdi's own health declined, too; he developed a number of physical infirmities that affected his eyesight and his ability to walk.

In December 1900, Verdi traveled to Milan to spend the holidays with friends, including Teresa Stolz, a soprano who had sung the part of Leonora in the 1869 version of *La forza del destino*, Arrigo Boito, and the Ricordi family.

On January 21, 1901, he suffered a stroke while buttoning his coat in his room at the Grand Hotel. Immediately friends, fans, and interested parties came together inside the hotel, while a large, concerned crowd gathered outside. A priest delivered extreme unction, a sacrament in which the sick or dying person is anointed with oil. The deathwatch lasted five days as Verdi lingered, unconscious and unaware of anything around him. Finally he died on the morning of January 27. Italy's most famous composer was dead at eighty-seven.

Verdi wanted a simple funeral service without music or pageantry; this was conducted early the following morning. However, the small crowd began to sing "Va, pensiero" from *Nabucco* as a way of bidding the great man farewell. Later, when the remains of Verdi and his wife were moved from the small cemetery to the grounds of the Casa Verdi, there was a huge ceremony. This was complete with a choir eight-hundred strong, ministers of state, and a crowd of one-hundred thousand lining the streets as the coffins passed.

Giuseppe Verdi left behind a legacy of twenty-six operas (twenty-nine including the ones that were revised), many of which are still being performed today in the world's major opera houses. He changed the course of opera by adding a theatrical panache and musical intensity to dramatic stories. He was a symbol of Italian nationalism and hence a symbol of human freedom from oppressors and he influenced a generation of composers who followed in his wake. By not caving in to the demands of censors, he showed that an artist must always seek out the truth, never bending to the minds of bureaucracy.

As the great Italian poet Gabriele d'Annunzio wrote on the occasion of Verdi's death: "He wept and loved for all."

Timeline

1813   Born on October 10 in Roncole.

1824   Studies music with Ferdinando Provesi in Busseto.

1832   Travels to Milan, is refused admittance to the conservatory; studies with Vincenzo Lavigna instead.

1833   Sister Giuseppa dies at age seventeen.

1836   Marries Margherita Barezzi, daughter of patron Antonio Barezzi; becomes music master of Busseto.

1837   Daughter Virginia born on March 26.

1838   Son Icilio born on July 11; Virginia dies August 12.

1839   Moves to Milan; Icilio dies October 22; premiere of first opera, *Oberto*, at La Scala; meets soprano Giuseppina Strepponi.

1840   Wife dies June 18; second opera, *Un giorno di regno,* flops.

1842   *Nabucco* is a success at La Scala.

1843   *I Lombardi alla prima crociata* premieres.

1844   Premieres of *Ernani* and *I due Foscari.*

1845   Premieres of *Giovanna d'Arco* and *Alzira.*

1846   Premiere of *Attila.*

1847   Premieres of *Macbeth* and *I masnadieri*; *I Lombardi* reworked as *Jerusalem* for the Paris Opera; buys farm at Sant' Agata.

1848	Premiere of *Il corsaro*; fighting in Milan between Austrian Army and Milanese forces; the Austrians succeed in retaking the city.
1849	Premiere of *La battaglia di Legnano* in Rome and *Luisa Miller* in Naples.
1850	Premiere of *Stiffelio*.
1851	Premiere of *Rigoletto*; moves from Busetto to Sant' Agata.
1853	Premieres of *Il trovatore* and *La traviata*.
1855	Premiere of *Les vêpres siciliennes* for Paris Exhibition.
1859	Premiere of *Un ballo in maschera*; great political unrest in Italy; marries Strepponi on August 29.
1862	Premiere of *La forza del destino* in St. Petersburg.
1867	Premiere of *Don Carlo* in Paris.
1871	Premiere of *Aida* in Cairo.
1881	Premiere of the revised (and official version of) *Simon Boccanegra* at La Scala.
1887	Premiere of *Otello* at La Scala.
1893	Premiere of *Falstaff* at La Scala.
1895	Approves the beginning of work on his home, Casa Verdi, for musicians.
1897	Giuseppina Strepponi dies November 14.
1899	Casa Verdi (Casa di Riposo) opens.
1901	Suffers a stroke on January 21; dies six days later.

Sources

CHAPTER ONE: The Musician from Roncole

p. 16, "I wrote a wide variety . . ." Mary Jane Phillips-Matz, *Verdi: A Biography* (Oxford: Oxford University Press, 1993), 30.

p. 21, "I was fresh from my studies . . ." Ibid., 50.

p. 23, "Just as I thought . . ." Ibid., 69.

CHAPTER TWO: Tragedy and Triumph

p. 26, "I have been an impassive spectator . . ." Phillips-Matz, *Verdi*, 74.

p. 36, "successes have never made . . ." Franz Werfel and Paul Stefan, *Verdi: The Man in His Letters* (New York: L. B. Fischer, 1942), 101.

CHAPTER THREE: From Milan to Venice

p. 45, "The lungs cannot hold up . . ." Werfel and Stefan, *Verdi*, 118.

CHAPTER FOUR: Macbeth and Conflict

p. 54, "it makes me sound . . ." Phillips-Matz, *Verdi*, 177.

p. 54, "It is certain that the newspapers . . ." Ibid., 179.

p. 57, "insensitive, mean, demanding . . ." Ibid., 226.
p. 58, "accursed note," Werfel and Stefan, *Verdi*, 135.
p. 65, "Honour to these heroes . . ." Ibid., 138.

CHAPTER FIVE: Many Battles
p. 70, "This blessed, blessed, blessed . . ." Marcello Conati, ed., *Encounters with Verdi* (Ithaca: Cornell University Press, 1984), 147.
p. 72, "perhaps the greatest drama . . ." Ibid., 155.
p. 73, "My notes . . . " Werfel and Stefan, Verdi, 228.
p. 73, "I find it a very, very beautiful . . ." Ibid.
p. 73-74, "If you take away the sack . . ." Ibid.
p. 76, "separate himself in residence . . ." Conati, *Encounters with Verdi*, 170.

CHAPTER SIX: Prisoner of Paris
p. 79, "who knows what relationship exists . . ." Werfel and Stefan, *Verdi*, 263.
p. 83, "Then it was a fiasco . . ." Phillips-Matz, *Verdi*, 355.
p. 85, "most famous people," Ibid., 331.
p. 85, "I never asked to be among . . ." Ibid.
p. 86, "have written two or three operas . . ." Werfel and Stefan, *Verdi*, 289
p. 90, "In any other place . . ." Phillips-Matz, *Verdi*, 346.

CHAPTER SEVEN: The Force of Destiny
p. 92, "I want to remain . . ." Phillips-Matz, *Verdi*, 344.
p. 97, "But what can I do . . ." Conati, *Encounters with Verdi*, 212.
p. 99, "rests the future greatness . . ." Werfel and Stefan, *Verdi*, 336.
p. 100, "I have not campaigned . . ." George Martin, *Verdi: His Music, Life and Times* (New York: Dodd, Mead, 1963), 377.

p. 103, "It was not a success . . ." Martin, *Verdi*, 353.

p. 103, "You can just imagine . . ." Ibid., 423.

p. 104, "You know . . ." Ibid., 432.

CHAPTER EIGHT: The Genius of Twilight

p. 106, "This is more than an inconvenience . . ." Werfel and Stefan, *Verdi*, 350.

p. 106, "I have carried your name . . ." Ibid.

p. 109, "Much *verve* but without . . ." Martin, *Verdi*, 364.

p. 110, "Here's to the health . . ." Ibid., 337.

p. 112, "Our music is different . . ." Conati, *Encounters with Verdi*, 237.

p. 117, "Great grief does not . . ." Martin, *Verdi*, 557.

p. 118, "He wept and loved for all," Ibid., 572.

Bibliography

Conati, Marcello, ed. *Encounters with Verdi*. Ithaca: Cornell University Press, 1984.

Cross, Milton. *The New Milton Cross' Complete Stories of the Great Operas*. New York: Doubleday, 1955.

Holden, Amanda, ed. *The Viking Opera Guide*. New York: Penguin Group, 1993.

Martin, George. *Verdi: His Music, Life and Times*. New York: Dodd, Mead, 1963.

Phillips-Matz, Mary Jane. *Verdi: A Biography*. Oxford: Oxford University Press, 1993.

Schonberg, Harold C. *The Lives of the Great Composers*. New York: W. W. Norton, 1970.

Werfel, Franz and Paul Stefan. *Verdi: The Man in His Letters*. New York: L. B. Fischer, 1942.

Web Sites

http://www.giuseppeverdi.it/Inglese/default.asp
This official Web site of Giuseppe Verdi claims to hold a treasure trove of information on the maestro in both Italian and English, and it does. It features a biography, portraits, a chronology, celebrations, and Verdi's discography, as well as information about his works, librettos, librettists and even travel tips for anyone interested in visiting the composer's birthplace in Italy.

http://www.operaitaliana.com/autori/autore.asp?ID=1
Opera Italiana offers visitors to this site a biography, images, personal letters, an autobiographical account of the beginning of Verdi's career and the creation of Nabucco, as told to Giulio Ricordi, and it links to a section called "curiosities," which details Verdi and the piano, Verdi and gastronomy, and Verdi as seen by Boito. For a fee, visitors can also listen to his musical compositions.

http://www.musicaltimes.co.uk/archive/obits/190103verdi. html
Two months after Verdi's death, the *Musical Times*, the United Kingdom's oldest classical musical journal, published the "In memoriam" article that appears on this site. The lengthy, March 1901 article provides some interesting reading.

Index